BLESSINGS THROUGH THE YEARS

Del Aven

Illustrations by
Debra Aven Swartzendruber

A LITTLE BIT OF 'THIS AND THAT'

Stories for the young, old, and all in between:
The Great Depression, Country Store, Tornado, Sheriff,
Caregiver, Adoption, Grandmother, Ole Miss, Empty Nest,
Christmas, Humorous Stories, and much more.

WINTERS
PUBLISHING

winterspublishing.com

Blessings Through The Years

Front Cover Photo and Illustrations © 2014 Debra Swartzendruber
Cover Concept: Debra Swartzendruber
Cover Design: Rachel Winters
Interior Design: Tracy Winters
Special thanks to Abbey Swartzendruber for her assistance.

Photos courtesy of Del Aven, Debra Swartzendruber, and other members of
        the family, unless otherwise credited.
Shall We Gather at the River? lyrics on page 74 by Robert Lowry.
Photos on the upper left and upper right of page 117 are used courtesy
        of *The Oxford Eagle*.
The Wolf Credo on Page 195 is used by permission. Copyright by
        Del Goetz & Associates, 1988; renewed 2013.
Photo on page 250 courtesy of Wil Howie.
Count Your Blessings lyrics on page 256 by Johnson Oatman, Jr.

Published by:
Winters Publishing
P.O. Box 501
Greensburg, IN 47240
www.winterspublishing.com
812-663-4948

ISBN 10: 1-883651-73-5
ISBN 13: 978-1-883651-73-2

Library of Congress Control Number: 2014951774

Printed in the United States of America.

Dedication

To my devoted husband, Russ,
of 60 years

To my precious daughter, Debra, and family,
John, Abbey, and Gracie Swartzendruber

To my precious son, Anson Abbe Aven, my sister,
Myra, Mother and Daddy Barber, and other loved ones
who have made it home before me—we will have a wonderful
and glorious reunion one of these days.

God bless you
Del Aven
Debra Swartzendruber
Abbey and Gracie

Numbers 6:24-25

Table of Contents

Thy word is a lamp unto my feet, and a light unto my path.
Psalm 119:105

Introduction

In My Time

My times are in Your hand; ...
—Psalm 31:15

I will bless the LORD at all times; ...
—Psalm 34:1

My, how the time goes by! There is no way that I can mention even a small portion of the blessings I have received or the changes in the world in my lifetime. I was born October 5, 1928, the year before the stock market crashed and the beginning of the Great Depression. Banks closed and millions of people were out of work. This was our country's worst business crash in its history. People sold apples on the street and many ate in soup kitchens to survive.

Of course, I was too young to know any of these troubles, but in the 1930s, I began to hear and see some of this unfolding in our family and community. During these years of depression, the Lord's blessings brought us through these times and other storms in our lives.

It was in 1939 that a worldwide conflict began. On December 7, 1941, the Japanese bombed Pearl Harbor in Hawaii and Congress soon declared war on Japan, Germany, and Italy.

From the time I was born in 1928 until today, 2014, I have lived under the leadership of fifteen presidents of the great United

States of America. John Calvin Coolidge was the president when I was born, followed by Herbert Hoover. In the 1930s, we didn't know much about the presidents and what was going on in the world because news traveled so slowly. We didn't have a radio or telephone, and news only came from friends or relatives by word of

Del's Underwood typewriter.

mouth. They would go into town and bring back to us the news that they heard.

At eighty-five years of age, this is a late but good time in my life to write some of my memories of days and years gone by. Some of these were written for my two precious grandchildren, Abbey, fourteen, and Gracie, eleven years old, who were adopted into our family from China. They often ask their granddaddy and me to tell them stories about our childhood.

For years I have intended to write about my life during the depression years, and life around a country store. There are also so many other memories of my early life, marriage, our two children, Debra and Anson, growing up in Oxford, Mississippi, and going to Ole Miss. I started writing a journal in the late 1960s, and have continued my journaling until the present. Some of these memories have been written and stored away for years. I occasionally read some of these journals and see the many prayers that have been answered.

Intermittently during the last ten to fifteen years, I have helped care for some of my precious loved ones and my writing and reading has been limited. What a blessing it was to be a caregiver for them and do what I could to meet their needs. Our family has been such a "close-knit" family for all the generations that I can remember. I have been so wonderfully blessed with a loving Christian family.

When my daughter, Debra, was at Ole Miss working on her MFA in Design, I wrote two children's books that she illustrated. A few years later, I typed and worked with my husband on a devotional book that was published by B&H Publishing Group. I was under contract to do other children's books for them, but family and children took priority at that time. I did occasionally write some articles for Christian magazines. Recently, I read a couple of books that inspired me to write again.

God has blessed me in so many ways during these many years. I pray for some more years so I can be a blessing to others. And now I want to share—

A LITTLE BIT OF THIS AND THAT

for the young, for the old, and all those in between.

And now for the rest of the story!

If I Dare

by

Del Aven

If I dare to write a story
Of what I see or hear,
May it tell of love and goodness,
Instead of hate and fear.

If I dare to plant a garden
Among the weeds and grass,
May I keep it clean and growing
For all of those who pass.

If I dare to paint a picture
In the sunshine or the shade,
May I always mix my colors
So that none will ever fade.

If I dare to sing a song
Of faith or hope or love,
May I hear an echo,
Directing from above.

1

Depression Years— Living in the Country

But seek first the kingdom of God and His righteousness, and all these things shall be added to you. —Matthew 6:33

We lived in the country in north Mississippi, about eight miles from the nearest town. Even though we lived in the country, with no means of transportation except by a wagon and mules, we were still probably better off than the city folks. We always had plenty of food since we raised most of it. Some of the time we didn't have any money.

The house we lived in was rented along with the land. Daddy was a sharecropper. He had to pay by giving a certain percentage of the crop that he made during the year. We had cows for milk, chickens for eggs and meat, and hogs also for meat. We had dried peas and apples, peanuts, potatoes, canned tomatoes, and always fresh vegetables from our garden in the spring through the fall. Also Daddy would go squirrel hunting occasionally and come home with two or three. Squirrel stew was a dish we all enjoyed.

My sister was born with a heart defect and was not healthy her first years. Of course, we didn't know what was wrong, because very rarely did we go to the doctor. Mother put Myra on a pallet in

(Below) The Barber family. Forest holding Myra, and Ora with baby Del.

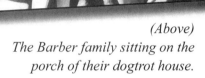

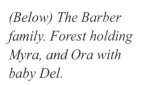

(Above) The Barber family sitting on the porch of their dogtrot house.

(Above) Del and Myra.

(Left) Myra, with her father, Forest Barber, and grandfather, James Jasper Barber.

the dogtrot porch of the house, and gave her a big red tomato to play with, while she worked in the garden. Myra was not old enough to roll off the pallet. Mother came to the porch to check on her and found she had eaten the entire tomato and had juice all over her little white dress. She had not been given any solid food up to this time and this really scared Mother. She suffered no ill effects from it, so Mother started feeding her solid food and she began to grow and gain weight.

Country living during the depression years required all of us to work. My mother and daddy instilled within Myra and me a strong work ethic. One of the jobs Myra and I had to do was to bring in wood for the kitchen stove. Once or twice we would forget, and all Daddy had to do was get the razor strap out. I don't ever remember him using the leather strap, but it sure scared us, and the fear of this punishment helped our memory. One night Myra and I had gone to bed and we heard thunder. We had forgotten to bring in the wood. He always wanted the wood in before a rain, because it was too hard starting a fire with wet wood. We lay there thinking what we should do. We decided we had to go out in the dark of night to get the wood in before it started raining. We eased out and went to the woodpile, but we made some noise when we came in with the wood. Daddy heard us and asked what we were doing. When we told him what had happened, he threw back his head and started laughing. We loved to hear our daddy laugh; it was just like music to our ears. We went to sleep in peace. He kidded us the next morning about our rambling around in the dark.

Hard Times

It was hard times making a living by farming in the 1930s. When Daddy had his crop work done, he would try to find another job. He got a job working on the road for 50 cents a day, paid by the government project known as the WPA. He took his mule and the road project furnished a large scoop. He would scoop up a heavy load of dirt one after the other all day. This was extremely hard work, but it paid for groceries that we did not have, such as salt, sugar, and flour, and also kerosene for our lamps and lanterns.

I remember our family going to a neighbor's house and shelling peas all afternoon. The shelled peas sold better in town than those in the hull. Myra and I were small children and got really tired after an hour or so. Mother could shell more peas than anyone there. When the shelling stopped, the peas were weighed and each person was paid. Myra and my peas were weighed. The man said we had each shelled enough to get nine cents. We waited patiently for our nickel and four pennies. He kept looking at his money and said he didn't have the right change. He said he only had dimes and would pay us when he got back from town. It was a sad time walking home without our money after working so hard.

We said, "Why couldn't he have just given us a dime?"!

We knew the value of even a penny.

One time, my aunt Dorothy (Harvey) Beeler told me she made 45 cents shelling peas. Taking her 45 cents to town, she bought three yards of material to make herself a dress. The material cost 5 cents a yard. She was very happy to have a new dress and 30 cents left over.

Pennies, nickels, and dimes could buy many things in those days. A double dip of ice cream was only a nickel. I remember very well the day we only got a single dip for a nickel. We were very disappointed.

Many people we knew were on what was called "Relief." The government would give clothes, food, and other items to needy people. My folks didn't want to take government aid and tried to get by without it. Anyway, one day our neighbors brought us a few of the "relief" things that they had received. One article of clothing was a little black-and-white-striped pair of coveralls that was a perfect fit for me. That was a wonderful and happy day—one I will never forget! Mother made most of our clothes from hand-me-downs; rarely did we ever get new or store-bought garments. Our underwear was made from salt and flour sacks.

When the crops were harvested, Daddy would start getting ready for winter. One of the big jobs was to cut enough kitchen stove wood and wood for the fireplace. One day his axe glanced off the chopping block and cut through his shoe, cutting three of his toes almost off. Mother had to run to a neighbor's house to get someone to take him to the doctor as quickly as possible, because he was bleeding very badly. They drove him to town and found a doctor. He sewed Daddy's toes back on with very little, if any, numbing medication. He said it almost killed him. He was not able to work for a long time.

Myra and I were small children, but we helped Mother all we could, taking care of the livestock, chickens, and other chores around the house and barn. We had some wonderful neighbors who also helped us during the cold winter months. Daddy did get well and was able to start his crop and farm work in the spring.

I remember when my grandfather, PaPa Harvey, as we called him, helped Daddy on the farm. They would be very tired at noon after getting up early each morning and going to work in the field. They would eat a big dinner and then stretch out on the dogtrot porch and take a nap before going back to plowing again.

Wash Day

Monday was usually the day we washed clothes. We filled a large black cast iron pot with water and built a fire around it. We put the white clothes in the pot first and let them boil. We took them out and put them in a number two tub. We then put the colored clothes in the pot to boil. I can see Mother standing in the backyard, with a broomstick in her hand, punching the clothes down in the pot. We had to get water from a well in the yard to fill the pot and tubs. After the clothes boiled and were in the tub, a rub board was used to scrub the clothes to be sure they were clean. Homemade lye soap was used in the wash water. One or two tubs of water were used to rinse the clothes, before hanging them in the sunshine on a barbed wire fence or a clothesline.

Myra and I always enjoyed playing in the rinse water. Mother would sometimes give us a "stick of blueing" to put in the rinse water. I never knew what it was for, but I think it was to make the white clothes look better. Wash day was always called "Blue Monday," so maybe that was part of the reason. Of course, Monday was the beginning of a new work week, and it was a hard week ahead.

We had a lot of dishcloths, towels, and washcloths to wash, which were really salt and flour sacks cut to fit the needs. Nothing was ever thrown away. We just didn't have garbage. The chickens and pigs ate the leftover food from the table. There were no tin cans, boxes, sacks, bottles, or paper to dispose of. If we had any paper, it was used to start fires in the kitchen stove or fireplace.

Those number two tubs also had another use. In the summer they were filled with water and placed in the sun to get warm. That was our bathtub, and we had fun playing in it. In the winter, water had to be heated on the stove or fireplace. Getting a bath in a cold house was no fun. That was usually only once a week and that was on Saturday.

Chickens

We always had chickens, all sizes, some to eat and some to lay eggs. Mother would order about twenty-five or fifty baby chicks each spring from a catalog, and they would be delivered to our house by the mail carrier. It was a fun day for us when the little chicks came. We would feed and give them water and watch them run and play. Sometimes Mother would hatch the chicks by letting a hen set on the eggs for about twenty-one days. The mother hen took care of them until they got to be fairly big chicks. When a thunderstorm came up, we had to put the small ones in the chicken pen so they could go in the coop. Myra would get so upset when they went round and round, and not go into the pen. As the thunderstorm approached, the situation grew worse. I was small at this time, but I ran out to help Myra by blocking off the chicks, herding them into the pen entrance. I guess the trouble was worth it, because we liked chicken and dressing, chicken and dumplings, and fried chicken.

When the preacher came to eat with us, we always tried to have fried chicken. That was when I learned to like wings, necks, livers, and the gizzards. The adults liked the drumsticks, breast, and larger pieces. It didn't matter to me. I would eat most anything that Mother cooked.

Mother

Mother was a wonderful cook. She liked to please us with good food, especially sweets like coconut and chocolate pie, banana cake, bread pudding, and sweet potato pie. One day Mother made a delicious banana cake and put sliced bananas all over the top. She wanted to make it look really good because we had relatives coming. They came and visited a while before eating. When Mother went into the kitchen, she looked at her cake and didn't recognize it, because there was not one banana slice on top. One of the small children who had come had slipped into the kitchen and eaten every slice.

When Mother took a hot, juicy cake out of the oven, she would give us a piece right then. She didn't make us wait until we had eaten our dinner. She was one of the sweetest mothers anyone could have. She loved us so much and we loved her just as much. There wasn't anything Mother asked of me that I wouldn't try to do to the best of my ability.

We would pick wild blackberries which we liked to eat. Mother made blackberry jelly and cobbler pies. We would also pick wild plums, dewberries, and summer grapes along the side of the road or in the nearby woods. In the spring another food we ate was a leafy plant we called poke salad or poke. It was usually found along the creek bank. We would mix it with mustard or turnip greens for a tasty dish.

I was very unhappy when Mother got sick. She often had

migraine headaches during the hot summer months. We didn't have electricity; therefore, no fans. The only fan we had was what we called a funeral home fan, because they were given to us at funerals. I remember Mother going to the coolest place she had, and that was under a big oak tree in the front yard. I took the cardboard fan with the wooden handle and would fan Mother for hours, it seemed to me. She would get cooler and soon feel better. I would wet a bath cloth in the cold well water and put it on her head.

Rats!

One year rats got into the chicken house and killed several of our chickens. We declared war on rats. Dad would wait near a pile of wood at night and shoot them as they came out. We also set large rat traps.

One night Myra and I had gone to bed when we heard a noise and some bumping. We heard loud talking. Mother and Daddy had a broom and stick in their hands. We finally found out they were at war with a rat in the kitchen. It was not long until the activity came into the bedroom. We were under the cover watching the chase. All of a sudden, the rat jumped from a chair to a small table and then landed in our bed and went under the cover. We came out of that bed faster than we had ever moved before! Finally, the chase was over and they got the rat. It took us a while to settle down and go to sleep that night.

Boogeyman

Daddy would gather the corn crop in the fall and put it in the barn for the cows and mules to eat during the winter. Also we would shell it and Daddy would take it to the gristmill to get it ground into meal. We would sit around the fireplace at night and shell corn and tell stories or play guessing games. Cornbread was a very important food around our house. It was delicious with butter and sorghum molasses. Some nights when there was nothing else to eat, we would just have cornbread and milk.

One day Mother walked to the mailbox, while Myra and I sat by the fireplace to keep warm on this very cold day. Our house was not sealed. We could see the rafters and framework. The crosspieces of the two by fours were good places to store small items. The floor was no better. It was wood planks with lots of cracks in it. That day while Mother had gone to the mailbox, Myra was rocking in her small rocking chair.

She said to me, "Del, do you hear that?"

I said, "What?"

She explained to me that every time she rocked she heard a noise under the house. We listened and we heard nothing, but she rocked again and heard the noise. She was getting afraid.

She said, "I think it is the boogeyman!"

She told me to get down and look through the cracks in the floor. I did and told her that I didn't see anything under the house except the chickens pecking the corn out of the cracks in the floor. We had shelled the corn the night before and the chickens were having a feast on it. I finally convinced her that it was not the boogeyman. She was very happy when Mother got home.

I think she was remembering that she had heard someone say that if you rob a bird's nest, the boogeyman will get you. She was never told this by Mother or Daddy, but they did tell her not to put her hand in the bluebird's nest that was in a fence post in the pasture. We passed by it each day and she just couldn't resist looking in the nest one day. She couldn't see the eggs, so she eased her little fingers into the nest and brought out the most beautiful little blue egg. After looking at it a long time and upon returning it to the nest, she broke it and the yolk went down her white dress. When she got to the house Mother asked her what was on her dress; she told the truth and said she was sorry, and she would never do that again.

The chickens enjoyed the corn and the boogeyman was never talked about again.

Medicine and Health Problems

During the 1930s people were bitten by mosquitoes and got malaria. It caused chills and fever. Mother had it once and was very sick. It was treated with quinine. One time my folks thought I was coming down with malaria. Daddy went to town and came back with Grove's Chill Tonic for Children. What a dose it was! It was bittersweet and it made me feel awful. We couldn't go outside in the late afternoon or night. Mosquitoes were feared. One summer I remember having a mosquito net over our bed at night for extra protection because they would come in the house. The buzzing in my ear was no fun to hear in the middle of the night.

When we got a cold, Mother rubbed our chest with Vicks Salve and heated a cloth and put it around our neck. We didn't mind that because it made us breathe better.

There was some medicine that I took as a child and I said, "When I grow up I will never take that medicine again!"

I can't recall ever going to a doctor when I was a small child. One day I thought I might have to go to one. One very cold day, my daddy and a friend were standing near our wagon in the yard. I went out to join them and see what they were talking about. There was a heavy frost on the wagon wheel, and it looked so good that I decided that I would lick it. I did, and my tongue stuck to the wheel, and it would not come off. I began to grunt real loud because I couldn't holler. Daddy saw my dilemma, and he and his friend couldn't decide what to do. He ran to tell Mother, and she came rushing out with some warm water and gently poured it on my tongue. What a welcome relief when my tongue was unattached and free. I never stuck my tongue to a wagon wheel again!

Daddy had lots of sore throats and tonsillitis. One time he was seriously ill. He contacted a surgeon and made an appointment to have his tonsils taken out. We were older children at this time, and Daddy talked to the doctor about us having our tonsils out at the same time. He said he didn't want us to get sick like he had been. Finally, the doctor and Daddy agreed it would be best to take them out. Mother reluctantly gave in, but Myra and I thought it was an awful decision. We begged and pleaded, but to no avail.

The day came and we went to the hospital, which looked like a big two-story house. I had never been to a hospital and didn't know what to expect. I wanted to be tough and brave, so I was taken first. I was put to sleep with ether. The doctor told me to start counting. The ether made me feel like I was going down a hill faster than I had ever traveled before. I think I got to the bottom of the hill when I couldn't count anymore. I knew nothing else until I woke up in the room.

When the doctor brought me in his arms down the steps to the room, Daddy looked at his little girl, all pale and limp. He said later that at that time he almost backed out of having the surgery for himself and Myra. I soon woke up, and the doctor proceeded with the other two surgeries. What a sore throat I had, but the ice cream they gave me later in the day helped so much. We all survived! We did get a sore throat sometimes, but, of course, no tonsillitis. We would have colds and fever at times. Mother always said, "Stuff a cold and starve a fever."

These are a few of the memories I have of my early years during the Depression. We went through many valleys, but there were also many happy and good times with our friends and loved ones. God supplied our needs and He was there to help us climb our mountains.

And my God shall supply all your need according to His riches in glory by Christ Jesus.   *—Philippians 4:19*

But those who seek the LORD shall not lack any good thing.
                                                    —Psalm 34:10

2

Christmas Forever

It was a Christmas in the early 1930s, during the Depression—a Christmas I will not forget. Times were hard for my parents, but as a child I didn't know it. I thought everyone lived like we did, except one of our neighbors who had a car. Daddy's only means of transportation was a wagon and two old mules. We had plenty to eat with what we had on the farm. We didn't always have things

Del and Myra.

like sugar, flour, and salt. Sometimes when Daddy went to town to get some of these items, he would buy us some cheese, cornflakes, a stick of peppermint candy, and maybe some Dubble Bubble gum. Mother would cut the bubble gum into four pieces and give it to my sister and me on special occasions. We made it last a long time, and sometimes Mother would find it stuck on the bedpost.

My mother was such a loving and caring mother, desiring always to see her two children have joy and happiness. She heard of a Christmas party in Water Valley, a small town about eight miles from where we lived. She said this party was for special children. I guess that meant children who were special like us.

Santa Claus would be there—and we had never seen Santa, only heard of him. Mother and Daddy taught us the real meaning of Christmas. Mother read the Bible to us often and told us that Christmas was when Jesus was born.

There would be a movie at this party, and we had never been to a movie. After the movie, Santa would give out stockings filled with—well, I didn't know—but I began to dream and hope for all kinds of things.

The problem now was getting a ride into town and getting tickets to get in the movie house (theater). In December in the 1930s the weather was extremely cold, too cold to ride into town in a wagon.

Somehow, Mother got the tickets and our neighbor would take us in his car. When Mother told us about all this, Myra and I jumped and leaped for joy. I can still remember how we jumped from one bed to the other. We had trouble going to sleep that night. The feeling deep inside was one I will never forget!

Finally, the long winter night passed, and we were bundled up for our cold, but exciting, ride into town. Even in a car it was cold; only flaps covered the windows, and, of course, there was no heater.

Upon arriving at the theater, the first person I saw was a girl who lived near us. She was almost grown. I thought, and always believed, Santa only gave gifts to children. There were lots of children and mothers lined up ready to go in the theater. I thought they would never start going in. My feet were so cold from the ride and also standing outside in this line. I always had cold feet, and I remember how Mother would heat a smoothing iron in the fireplace at night, wrap it in a towel or small blanket, and put it to my feet when she tucked me in bed each night.

We finally got to the door, and the man reached for the tickets Mother was holding. He looked at them and then said to Mother, "Lady, these are not the right kind of tickets to get in—you suppose' to have special tickets. This party is just for special children." I couldn't believe we were not special children!

Mother, being the kind of mother she was, couldn't bear to think that we had come this far and would not be able to get in. No one could know the disappointment I felt inside. I said nothing, but big tears rolled down my face. The man looked down at us, and then to our mother, and said, "Go see Mr. Eddie over at the bank across the street—he might have some more special passes."

We could hear the music coming from the front of the theater and we knew the movie had begun. We hurried across the street to the bank, and Mother asked for Mr. Eddie. Mother told us Mr. Eddie was the most influential man in town and probably the most "well-to-do."

We felt so small, standing in this big bank, asking for the top person in the entire town. Soon, Mr. Eddie came in. He was a kind-looking man, and he looked down at us and smiled. Mother told him what had happened and how disappointed we were. He looked at us again and said, "Wait just a minute."

He went behind the counter, asked what our names were, and wrote something on a piece of paper, handing it to Mother. He said, "Just give this to them at the door—they will let you in, don't want anyone to miss Santa—Merry Christmas!"

We got in and began to watch our first movie. Our unhappy experience soon turned to joy and excitement. The large theater, soft seats, large screen, even the bright electric lights were all so new to us, and we sat there trying to absorb it all.

Would Santa Claus really be there? I was beginning to wonder. When the movie ended, the lights came on brighter, and through the side door out jumped Santa, with a huge bag across his shoulders. After a few "Ho, Ho, Ho's and Merry Christmas," he began to call out names. One by one the children went down to meet him face-to-face, and receive a stocking stuffed with what looked like fruit, candy, and toys. My neighbor, the big girl, went down for her stocking. I had plenty of time to watch her admiring her gifts. Santa's bag was getting smaller and smaller. It appeared at times to be empty. Would he have a stocking for my sister and me? Did he have our names on his list? I imagine my mother was sitting there praying all this time that we wouldn't be disappointed again.

Finally, he called our names, and we walked together down the long aisle to receive our long-awaited gift from Santa, himself, face-to-face for the first time.

What a joy this was! It was worth the waiting. Santa reached into his bag and pulled out the last two stockings and handed them to us. We looked up at his face and thanked him. The apple, the orange, a few nuts, a stick of peppermint candy, a small tin flute, and a few more things were all enjoyed for many days, but the memory has lasted a lifetime.

Today, most of us have loved ones who are not with us, who have already met the Lord face-to-face. Their names were written in the Book of Life. They knew Jesus as their Savior, received their rewards, and will live in Heaven, where it will be Christmas forever.

As in those years gone by, Mr. Eddie was the man who wrote our names down and gave us that pass for us to enter that childhood joy. May we help others to receive their special pass through Jesus Christ—which is the only way into eternal life—into unspeakable joy—forever!

May we at Christmastime and always, be willing to share our material and spiritual blessings with a world in need—even if it means cutting our bubble gum into four pieces!

God gave us the greatest gift ever—Jesus Christ, His Son, our Savior. This is the meaning of Christmas Forever!

Every good gift and every perfect gift is from above, and comes down from the Father of lights, ...   —*James 1:17*

Myra, Del, Forest (Daddy), and cousins.

3

School

A group of students in front of the O'Tuckolofa School in the 1920s.

I was born in a small three-room house about five miles from the nearest town. The house had a kitchen, living room-bedroom combined, and a storage room. It did have a front porch. The best thing about growing up here was that we could walk to church, school, and Granny Harvey's house. We could see all three from our front porch.

Before we were old enough to go to school, we enjoyed watching the schoolchildren play. When we played outside, Mother checked on us often as she did her work. One day she came to check on us, and Myra was nowhere to be found. Mother looked everywhere around the house and barn. She was getting frantic over her lost child. She told me to come with her to look at the school.

We went in the first door we came to, which was the first grade classroom. Sitting there in the reading circle was Myra. She was enjoying every minute of it. The class, however, was temporarily interrupted as Mother came in, talked to the teacher, apologized, and made a quick exit with Myra. She was reprimanded later, I'm sure, but Mother was so happy to have her lost child in her arms, that she was also given hugs and love.

In a year or two, we moved to another house several miles from the school. Myra was now old enough to go to school, but she had to ride the school bus. This was a sad day for Mother and me, to have her away from us all day. I didn't have my playmate anymore,

(Above) O'Tuckolofa teachers in the 1930s.

(Right) Del's cousin, Bobby Gene Blount, in front of the O'Tuckolofa School.

and I missed my sister so much. We lived off the main road, so Mother and I had to walk her to the bus in the morning and meet her again in the afternoon.

I'll Never Learn to Read

One day Myra came home from school with her first book and had a reading assignment. This was not a good day. How vividly I remember Mother and Myra sitting on the porch going over the words and story. I can see and hear them going over the lesson as if it were today.

Myra began to cry, "I'll never learn to read, I'll never learn to read, I don't know Dan from Tan."

By looking on the best I could, I figured out that Dan was the boy and Tan was the dog.

My big sister did learn to read, and eventually became valedictorian of her high school senior class. She had to give a talk at the graduation ceremonies.

She said, "I can't do it! I just can't get up before everyone and give a speech!"

She did, however, and made a great speech. She went on to get a BAE, MAE, and an Advanced Masters Degree in Reading. She taught Reading Improvement at Northwest Community College and was Supervisor for Ole Miss practice teachers. She taught a total of thirty-five years. Most of these years were in public schools.

Now to Him who is able to do exceedingly abundantly above all that we ask or think, according to the power that works in us,
—Ephesians 3:20

More School Problems and Praise

Getting back to another time in Myra's early school days was when she got very sick. For several weeks she missed school, and finally, it was decided that she had red measles when she broke out in a rash. She was very weak for a long time. After a lengthy period of time, Mother and Daddy decided she was well enough to go back to school.

We were anxious all day wondering how she was making it at school. Mother and I went to the road early that afternoon to wait on the bus to come. Finally, the bus came; one child got off and we waited, looking for Myra, but she was not on the bus. Since she had been sick for so long and was not riding the bus, the driver may have forgotten her, or else she may have been late getting to the bus. Anyway, Mother was really worried and upset. The bus driver told us to get in the bus, and after taking another child home, he would drive us to the school. How relieved and elated we were to see Myra in good hands with her teacher. For whatever reason, she had been left at school and was very upset! The stress of our lost or missing child on one hand, and the fear of being left behind on the other, melted away as we were reunited again.

My sister did not like school in the third and fourth grades, because of the multiplication tables. The teacher put the numbers in an imaginary fishbowl, and they had to fish out the answers in some sort of a game. She went to school crying many mornings, not wanting to eat and nauseated. Daddy went to the school to talk to the teacher to see what could be done to help her. Daddy told Mother something must be done soon, because these multiplication tables were just about to cause him to lose his crop. She soon learned the math by another method, and from then on school was better.

My precious sister was my mentor, who helped me many times in my schoolwork and throughout my life.

Myra was incapacitated by a stroke for several years before her death. I often took her with me, and she would sit in the car while I shopped. Friends would often stop and talk with her. One day one of her fourth-grade students, who she hadn't seen in many years, stopped and talked with her. The former student said she had just retired after teaching thirty years. She said Miss Barber

(Myra) was one of the reasons she became a teacher. She said she had encouraged many of her own students to become teachers. She thanked Myra for being one of her best teachers. Many times I have heard her students tell her she was their best teacher, and many other compliments, and praise was given to her.

I can't remember much about my early years in school. I didn't mind going, and I especially liked recess. Don't most children! I liked the games and especially softball. When the boys chose teams, girls were usually chosen last, because they couldn't bat the ball. I was always elated when I was chosen even before some of the boys. The boys liked to have me on the team because I could hit the ball, and occasionally even hit a home run.

When I was in the fifth or sixth grade, I remember that we had to memorize many things. We memorized all the presidents, states and capitals, counties of our state, governors of our state, and many poems. If we were disobedient or talked too much, we had to stay in at recess and memorize other things. Some of these have been remembered through the years and used. After Myra had her stroke, the therapist asked her questions to check her memory, such as adding or subtracting numbers. She then asked Myra if she knew the first three Presidents of the United States. I was sitting there with a smile on my face because I knew the therapist would be in for a surprise. Myra started saying the Presidents, and she finally had to stop her after about ten or fifteen. We all had a good laugh. Having a good memory is a blessing! Myra had such fun telling stories about going to a country school, her teaching days and what she had learned. Those memories helped her cope with being in a wheel chair. Myra liked memorizing the Bible too. It is a blessing that God keeps us in His memory and it is He …

Who remembered us in our lowly state,
For His mercy endures forever;
—Psalm 136:23

O'Tuckolofa School reunion pictures through the years.

4

The Country Store

Del's family with O'Tuckolofa teachers in front of the country store.

Mother didn't like for Myra to ride the school bus and wanted to move back closer to the school. She kept recalling the day the bus had left her child at school. I would also be going to school the next year. Daddy was able to find some land to farm and could rent the small house near the school where we had lived before. This was the house where I was born.

We could now see Myra walk to school and playing outside at recess. She could come home for lunch. These were good days.

We had good friends, and best of all, we now lived near Granny and PaPa. We would walk there almost everyday. Granny always had something good to eat, especially fried apple pies.

We were now close to the church, and we could go more often than when we lived at the other house. We were living here when Daddy made a profession of faith in Christ and joined the church. I think he believed, but just had not joined a church. Mother had made this decision when she was a child. I am so thankful that Myra and I grew up in a Christian home, with a mother and father who loved the Lord. We also had both maternal and paternal grandparents living near us at this time, who had guided our parents in the way they should live when they were growing up.

At this time we didn't have a means of transportation, except for the wagon and mules. The five miles to town in the wagon was a very tiring trip for me as a child.

Daddy was not making enough money farming to meet the needs of his family, so he thought up a way to supplement it. He asked the O'Tuckolofa School trustees if he could lease some land that the school owned, which was not being used by the school. They agreed to do so for ten dollars a year. Daddy was going to step out on faith and build a country store.

He went to Water Valley and found an old house that was partially burned and paid $17.50 for it. He had to tear it down and move it to the school location. I don't know how he got it moved, probably by wagon and mules, or by someone who had a truck.

Daddy met a relative in town that day and Daddy told him what he was planning to do.

He looked at Daddy, and said, "Forest, you are going to lose every thing you have doing that. You can't make it in a country store."

He came home that day, laughing about what the relative had said. He told Mother that if he lost it all, it wouldn't be much, because he didn't have much invested. It wasn't long until Daddy started his new adventure.

He built a large room that would be the store. Behind this were two more rooms which were the living room-bedroom and the kitchen. With the $50.00 he had left, he bought items for the store. He stocked items most needed by country folks and supplies used at school. The schoolchildren could walk to the store at recess and lunch hour for their paper, pencils, apples, and other supplies. Some children would bring eggs to exchange for school supplies, such as a cedar pencil or a Blue Horse notebook.

Daddy didn't have a cash register. He used a cigar box to keep his money in and put it under the counter when not in use.

We got a better lamp to use in the store. It was a brighter light than the kerosene lamp we had used all our life. It had a tall globe on it. One night Daddy put it on a high shelf and it caught the ceiling paper on fire. That really scared us, because all the water that we had was a bucket of water and a dipper in the kitchen. We had to draw more water from a bored well in the backyard. Daddy and some people that were in the store put the fire out before too much damage was done.

It was a great day when Daddy opened the store for business. It was slow at first, but the more items he added, the more business he had. Daddy bought a small car that he needed to get goods from town for the store. At this time there was not a wholesale route in the county. Later on, a salesman would come to the store every week, take orders of things we needed, and deliver them in a few days.

Storms and Rain

The store was built near a small creek with a culvert under the road. In 1936, a bad storm came with much rain. We were very much afraid we would be blown away. The thunder and lightning were awful. We looked out the door and the water had overflowed the creek banks, and the yard was flooded. Daddy started getting items in the store off the floor and gathering items in the house area. The water almost got to the floor. We found out later that this was the storm that produced a tornado in Tupelo, Mississippi. Much of the town was destroyed and many people were killed.

Another day we had a flash flood and the water got up to the floor. We heard the chickens making a loud noise. Daddy knew they were under the house and about to drown. He got his crowbar and started pulling up the floor. He got out several chickens and took them to higher ground.

One of our neighbors was also afraid of storms. She begged us to join her family and go to the school building when there was a storm approaching in the night. She said the building was storm-sheeted and safer than our houses. I never knew what that meant. A few times we did meet her family there. I was still a small child, and it was so hard getting up in the middle of the night and walking up the hill to the school. There were lots of windows in the school auditorium and the lightning was frightening. Mother and Daddy didn't think this was a safe place to go, so we decided to stay in the store from then on.

More Store Stories

The principal of the school was a good man and a fun person to be around. He and Daddy were always kidding each other. Many afternoons after school, we could see him coming down the hill toward the store. We knew he was coming to play checkers with Daddy. They had a checkerboard, but no checkers. Coke caps served perfectly for the checkers, and they laughed and had more fun sitting there on the nail kegs, playing this classic game.

A neighbor lady came in the store one day while they were playing. She had on a sweater that had holes all over it—really worn out.

The principal looked at her and said, "You better not sneeze, because if you do, your sweater is going to fall off!"

They often kidded each other, and the woman with the worn-out sweater and the principal both had a good laugh. Everyone was poor, and no one worried about what anyone had to wear.

After the checker game was over, he picked up his rope and said he had to go to pasture and get his cow. Before he left, Daddy asked him if he wanted some muscadine juice. He drank it and asked for another glass full. Daddy told him it was pretty strong, like wine, and he'd better not drink anymore. The principal insisted it would not hurt him. Daddy said he had let it 'set' too long. The man drank it and went on to get his cow. When he came back, he was staggering and dropped his rope. He was all bent over, trying to find it. I heard Daddy start laughing, saying he had told him not to drink that other glass. They both had a big laugh the next day. Daddy never made the muscadine grape "juice" again. No alcoholic beverages were ever in our house.

There were at least two people who got drunk in our community. One man would get so loud at his home, we could hear him hollering at his family all the way to our house. Sometimes when Dad was away from the store, Mother would lock the door, and we would go to the barn or in the woods when we thought he would stop at the store. We would watch him drive down the road from one side to the other.

One night he came, but Dad was in the store. He started talking bad. Daddy told him that he was going to have to stop that kind of talk, because his family lived in the back of the store. This made the man mad.

He said, "I want some sardines and crackers, and I want to eat them right now."

Daddy gave him a can of sardines and put some crackers in a sack, and told him he'd better go on home.

He shouted real loud, "You don't want me in here!"

He took the sack and got in his topless car, with a steering wheel that had only two spokes. He had wrecked it several times.

He turned as fast as he could in the middle of the road. He threw the sack out of the car, scattering the sardines and crackers down the road behind him.

Snake in the Ceiling

On another occasion Daddy was gone and Mother, Myra, and I were taking care of the store. I looked up in the ceiling and saw something moving under the building paper that covered the burned wood ceiling. As I mentioned earlier, the store was built out of a partially-burned house. Anyway, mice would get in between the building paper and the ceiling wood. When Daddy heard or saw some movement overhead, he knew it was a mouse. He would stop the mouse, cut a small slit in the paper, find the tail, pull it through, and throw it to the floor.

This was a new experience for me to get rid of another mouse in the ceiling. I stopped the movement and hollered to Mother, "I've got a mouse."

I was in a chair trying to hold the wiggling mouse. I started feeling the bulge in the paper to try to find the tail—something was wrong.

I called Mother, "Look, it's this long."

This scared Mother, because she and I both were afraid of snakes. This was a dilemma. She didn't want the snake to bite me, which was unlikely under the paper, but she also didn't want the snake to get loose in the ceiling. She told me to hold on in the middle of it and she would get something to hold it. She got the metal shoe last and gave it to me. I was standing in a chair and the metal tool, used for shoe repair, was getting very heavy.

A traveling salesman was outside the store, so Mother ran and asked him if he would come and help us kill a snake. Mother ran back in the store to hunt a hammer or ax, or something to kill the snake. I was about to give out, holding the shoe last, so Mother wasted no time in working on the snake. When we thought we had things under control, Mother went to see where the salesman was. He was not to be seen anywhere. I guess he was more afraid of snakes than we were. Mother took care of the snake, but we often laughed about the runaway salesman.

We found a good way to control the snakes around our area. One day we were happy when a stray cat came to our store. We kept this cat, and named her "Tab." She was a good cat and was not afraid of snakes. She killed all the snakes that came near our house. We watched her kill some. She was not only good at killing snakes; one day we were surprised to see that she came home with a rabbit in her mouth.

All the Candy You Want

It is so tempting for children to have candy in sight at all times, and sometimes there were even new kinds of candy in the store—so tempting. We were limited as to how often we could have candy.

I remember Myra telling Daddy one day, "I have never had all the candy I want!" She repeated this several times and begged to have more.

One day Daddy went in the store and got five or six big bars of candy and put them in her lap.

"Now, I don't want you to ever say you never had enough candy," he said.

She ate two or three and was slowing down pretty fast. She whispered to me, "I don't think I can eat another bite."

She never said she wanted more candy again.

We also liked vanilla wafers that came in a small box and contained fifteen round crispy wafers. We would get on the front porch of the store and divide the wafers evenly. Myra got exactly seven and a half and I got seven and a half. We always asked our parents' permission before we ate candy or cookies. They wanted us to be healthy and have good teeth, but candy and vanilla wafers were a rare treat and we made them last a long time, nibbling on the crisp cookies very slowly.

Living in the Store

There was no electricity, no inside water or bathrooms, no refrigerator, or telephone. We did have an ice box that would keep ice for a few days, if we could get the ice. There was a truck that soon began to deliver ice to the store. Daddy would buy fifty or a hundred pounds when they came. We began to sell cold soft drinks and we were able to have cold milk to drink.

We bought our first radio that had a battery. During the week at 6:30 each evening, Daddy turned the radio on to hear Lum and Abner at their Jot 'Em-Down Store. He never wanted to miss it, because it related a lot to his own country store. Sometimes the reception

Old Philco radio.

was bad because of certain weather conditions, and he would miss the program.

About the only problem that Mother and Daddy had between themselves was when he would sell on credit, and people would be unable to pay their bills. Mother knew they needed all the cash sales to be used to restock the store. Mother always seemed to know who could be trusted. Daddy probably knew also, but realized they were in need. Mother didn't want the store to be open on Sunday, which she said was the Sabbath Day, and needed to be kept holy. She would tell Daddy that people had six days to buy what they needed.

By living in the store, it was hard not to open when someone knocked on the door. A neighbor would come wanting aspirins for a sick child, and while the door was open, another neighbor would stop and want to buy a bottle of snuff. He wanted a bottle with four dots on the bottom. He said it was stronger and better than the bottles with only one, two, or three dots.

Very often, my job was selling a nickel's worth of kerosene, better known in those days as "coal oil." The old tank would get air in the pipes and spew and spray the stuff all over me. It smelled awful and was so hard to wash off.

The principal and teachers' home (provided by the school system for the principal, his wife, and several other teachers) was not very far from the store. One afternoon they left to go to a movie in town. Daddy and I decided to have some fun with them when they returned home. We made a dummy man, all dressed in clothes and a hat. We put a cigarette in its mouth and put it in front of the house. We left, but went back about the time we thought they would return. When Daddy saw the car coming, he lit the cigarette, and we hid.

They put the car in the garage and all of them came around the house, laughing and talking. Soon the laughter turned to silence, and they stopped immediately. The principal hollered, "Who are you? What are you doing here?"

There was still silence. One of the lady teachers took her high heel shoes off and was ready to run if she needed to. He hollered again, "If you don't talk to me, I'm coming over there!"

He walked closer to the dummy and realized the ploy. He put the cigarette out, and they all went in the house. We had fun, but never made our appearance that night. They probably knew immediately who was behind this set-up.

On another occasion, we had another laugh. The principal's house was very near the school. He was at school, forgot something, and returned to his house very unexpectedly. He found their maid on the back porch, brushing her teeth with his toothbrush. We kidded him, saying we wondered how long this had been going on! During these hard times, we used a toothbrush a long time. Sometimes we made a toothbrush out of a hickory stick and brushed with soda.

The store was an important place in that community. As I said, Daddy would open the store when people were in need. God was always there for us when we had needs and called on Him. He opened His storehouse for us and even in these hard times, I enjoyed the blessings of living in a country store, near the teacher's home, school, and church.

Blessed be the Lord,
Who daily loads us with benefits,
The God of our salvation! Selah
—Psalm 68:19

5

The Frozen Goldfish

It would soon be Christmas, my favorite time of the year. I always looked forward to this week, to be out of school and home with my family. My third-grade teacher asked me on the last day of school if I would take the classroom pet goldfish home and take care of it during the Christmas vacation. The students always felt honored to have the teacher ask them to do something for her. I felt this was a real honor. It was a typical goldfish bowl, with pretty gravel on the bottom, and only one beautiful goldfish swimming around and around in the bowl. I think it cost probably a penny or two, no more than a nickel. She gave me some food that looked like thick paper. I knew how to feed it, because she let the students feed it. We would watch it take the food into its mouth and spit it out again.

I took "Goldie" home with me. I was ever so careful not to drop the bowl as I walked home from school. We lived near the school, so we walked home, and didn't have to ride the school bus. I didn't know the thrill, honor, and excitement of this day would turn out to be a horrible Christmas for me and a devastating time of my life.

The weather was always cold from November until the end of February, but this particular Christmas was exceptionally cold. We only had a fireplace for heat in the living room, which also served as the bedroom. We also had a wood cookstove in the kitchen, which provided some heat in that area of the house.

I put Goldie on the mantel above the fireplace, because I thought this would be a warm, cozy place for the cold week ahead. Daddy would put a big log at the back of the fireplace, which would last a long time. Sometimes he would get up in the middle of the night and add more logs to the fire, to keep the house warmer, and not let the fire go out.

One morning I woke up and it was terribly cold. The temperature must have been down to zero. We didn't know, because we didn't have a thermometer. Dad got up and punched the fire to get it warm enough in the house for us to get dressed and start enjoying our Christmas vacation. My sister and I were looking forward to some gifts, candy, and Santa Claus.

I looked up at the goldfish bowl and Goldie was not moving. After a closer look, I could see that the water was frozen solid, and there was Goldie, with mouth wide open and those big eyes staring at me. This really let the wind out of my sails. I felt so depressed; I didn't know what to do. For the rest of the vacation days, the little goldfish remained encased in the ice. Christmas was always a wonderful, exciting time for me, a typical, jolly eight-year-old. Every time I looked at that bowl, there was Goldie looking back at me!

I asked Mama what I was going to do when the time came to go back to school. Mama always gave me good advice. She told me, with a hug around my neck, to take the goldfish back just like it was and give it to Miss Martha. That was an awful day, when I had to walk to school with that bowl of ice and the staring goldfish. I left early to be able to walk into Miss Martha's third-grade room before the bus got there. I wanted to avoid having the other children watch me walk in with my Christmas disaster.

I can't remember what Miss Martha said, but I'm sure it must have made me feel better. Just getting rid of the goldfish responsibility and having it out of the house was such a relief!

Sometimes in life, some of the things we think may bring us joy may only bring us distress and pain. It may be such a little thing in life that happens to us that puts us in a spin. We fret and worry, wondering what to do, or what the outcome will be. When stressful times seem to get the best of us, we need, more than ever, to keep our focus on the Lord. It is He who can calm our fears and lift us up. He can put the wind back in our sails and give us smooth sailing. Fear is a thief and can rob us of our joy. We must, however, call on Him and ask for His guidance, protection, and blessings, and thank Him for wise mothers and understanding teachers when there are frozen fish moments.

Peace I leave with you, My peace I give to you; not as the world gives do I give to you. Let not your heart be troubled, neither let it be afraid.   *—John 14:27*

6

Transportation
Tricycle, Bicycle, Car, and Truck

I had hoped and prayed for a bicycle for many years, and finally, one Christmas the long-awaited gift came—a beautiful blue bicycle. I was proud of this blue bike; it brought back memories of another Christmas long years before, when Myra and I got a red second-hand tricycle. China dolls, one for each of us, also came that day, along with the tricycle. These beautiful little dolls had a ceramic head with a soft cloth stuffed body. A few days later, Myra was peddling the tricycle, and I was standing up on the back behind her. We were taking our dolls for a ride in the kitchen, which was the

Del on her bicycle.

best place to ride. Myra turned a curve too fast, and down I went with a crash. It didn't hurt me, but my doll lay on the floor with the china head in several pieces. I was sorry this had happened, but I was not devastated. I never liked to play with dolls like Myra did. I would play dolls with her, if she would go outside and play ball or some other outside game.

On another occasion, I remember Myra peddling the blue bicycle, and I was sitting on the back fender, holding on to her. We often rode the bike about a mile down the gravel road to a friend's house to play. When we finished playing and left, Myra was peddling rather slowly. It was a very hot day and I was anxious to get home. I got off the bike and told her I was going to push her to get a good running start, which I did; then I jumped on the fender.

She began to wobble, and I fell off backwards. My head hit the gravel first, then my elbows and knees. I was not hurt seriously, but it was a day to remember.

One day Daddy came home with a second-hand "Model A" car. It was a small car with a front seat and a rumble seat in the back that was not enclosed. Sometimes Daddy would use the rumble seat to bring store items from town. Myra and I liked to take a ride in the rumble seat, with our hair blowing and the wind in our faces. It was to us then like a convertible is to young people today. One huge difference would be the cost. I wish I could remember how much my daddy paid for that Model A. It couldn't have been much. This little car was a wonderful means of transportation, compared to the wagon and mules.

One day we decided to go visit my grandparents, who lived a few miles from us. Daddy asked Mother if she would like to drive. She reluctantly got behind the wheel.

Mother was the type of person who enjoyed cooking, canning, sewing, and doing things in the house. She and Myra liked home activities better than dealing with anything mechanical. I followed in my daddy's footsteps. I loved the outdoors—working, hunting, shooting a rifle, and watching him fix things.

After Mother was seated comfortably behind the wheel, Daddy gave her some final instructions. Mother did fine keeping the car in the middle of the gravel road. There was not very much traffic during those days.

When we got near our granny's house, Mother missed the dirt driveway that was hidden by a dirt bank. As she went up the side of the bank, she mashed the accelerator instead of the brake. Daddy got his hand on the wheel, and before long, the car was under control. By this time, dust had covered the entire car. When it stopped, Mother rushed out to check on us. She looked to see if we were still in the rumble seat. Under a cloud of dust, she grabbed and hugged us to see if we were all right.

She said, "I thought I had killed my children."

We did have a good time visiting with Granny, PaPa, and Aunt Dorothy. When we got ready to leave, Daddy knew not to ask Mother if she wanted to drive. Mother never drove a car again in the sixty-eight years of her life.

Our next vehicle was a 1937 Ford pickup truck that Daddy needed to get groceries from town for the store. He also used it to take farm produce to Memphis and other towns. He let me drive it all over the fields to pick up peanuts, corn, hay, potatoes, and anything that needed to be picked up or moved. I was only nine years old, but I helped my daddy by driving the truck whenever there was a need. I remember when I was first allowed to drive Myra and Mother to Water Valley, a town about five miles away. This driving experience was fun; but I was concerned, because I was

just able to touch the brake and see over the steering wheel, while sitting on a pillow. This got better as I grew older.

When I was fifteen years old, we had a car. At this time we were living in town. There was a requirement that everyone had to have a driver's license. I walked to town from our house to the city hall, which was about one-fourth to one-half mile. They told me in the city hall that I had to have my parents sign for me since I was only fifteen. I got the papers, walked back home, and Mother signed them. I then walked back to city hall, gave them the signed papers, and handed them a quarter. They gave me my driver's license. I didn't have to take any kind of written or driving test.

Up until I was six and Myra was eight, we traveled by wagon pulled by mules. I can remember one of our mules was named Gabe. It took a long time to go into town, which was five miles away. Myra and I were so excited to go to town in the wagon! Then when we came back home, unloaded, and settled in for the night, everything was still and quiet except for the chorus of screech owls and crickets down by the creek. I fell asleep happy and safe. I didn't think there was any place I would rather be than right here in the country. I had never been on a plane or train or transported to faraway places, but to me at that time, I thought my greatest blessing was my family and O'Tuckolofa.

The LORD shall preserve your going out and your coming in
From this time forth, and even forevermore.
—Psalm 121:8

I will both lie down in peace, and sleep;
For You alone, O LORD, make me dwell in safety.
—Psalm 4:8

7

Who Spilled the Beans?

Country living had its ups and downs, but for the most part, it was wonderful during my early life. Going barefooted, wading in the creek, fishing, going squirrel hunting with my daddy, shooting a rifle, and riding my bicycle on the gravel road were some of the joys of summertime in the country. But it was not all fun and games, when Daddy said we had to plant potatoes in the early spring, or gather an acre of cucumbers, or hoe the grass out of the garden on a hot summer day.

It was such a day when Daddy said we had half an acre of black-eyed peas to plant. Mother, Myra, and I got our straw hats and made our way to the field, where Daddy had prepared the rows where we would plant the peas. We took our sack of peas and began to drop the peas a certain distance apart, as he had instructed us. Mother sometimes had to leave us and go take care of the store when she saw someone stop.

It was about noon, sweat got in my eyes, a gnat was trying to do the same, and then a sweat bee stung me. Sweat bees hurt, and besides that, I was hungry, as any eight-year-old would be about noon.

I sat down on a tree stump in the field, to cool a minute and wipe the sweat. Wiping sweat, swatting gnats, and balancing the pea sack did not work; somehow, my sack of peas spilled in the loosely-plowed ground around the stump. I got down on my hands and knees and picked up all the peas I could, which included dirt and trash. I finally gave up and covered the rest of the peas with the loose dirt. I didn't let them know why my sack of peas was so small. I was glad when Daddy said it was time to go home for dinner. Dinner was at noon and supper was at night in the country in Mississippi.

Mother had already gone home, so we knew she was cooking a good meal for us. We usually had a delicious dessert, which was my favorite part of dinner.

Weeks passed, and Daddy was plowing the peas, and we were hoeing. Daddy stopped his mule and looked at all the peas around the stump. I think he knew exactly what had happened.

He said, "Those peas are doing mighty good around that old stump. That soil will produce a lot of peas one of these days."

I just kept on hoeing, but Myra knew what I had done, and she was the one who "spilled the beans," so to speak. She told Daddy I was the one who dropped my sack and spilled the peas around the stump. That season there was a good stand of peas in all the rows, which was fortunate, because I was very nearsighted, and sometimes I would cut the peas down with the grass.

Anyway, Daddy had a great sense of humor, and a good personality—so he never reprimanded me for the bountiful crop of peas around the stump. Yes, I was the one who spilled the peas, but my sister, Myra, "Spilled the Beans!"

Just as the peas were covered with the soil, so it is with the sins we commit. They may be covered up, camouflaged, never told, and the world may never know, but God knows. There is no hiding from Him. Someday we will all stand before Him as an open book, to be held accountable for our deeds and sins.

Proverbs 28:13 says, "He who covers his sins shall not prosper, But whoever confesses and forsakes them will have mercy."

My father did not reprimand me for spilling the peas and covering them, because he knew my heart. I had pleaded guilty and told him I was sorry.

Jesus Christ covered all our sins when He died on the cross. We must confess our sins, repent and ask forgiveness, and believe in Him who died for us, rose the third day from the grave, and is alive today. He anxiously awaits with open arms those who will accept Him as their Savior. How blessed I was to have a forgiving earthly

father. But what a wonderful blessing it is to have a forgiving Heavenly Father, whether we spill the peas or the beans!

Who is a God like You,
Pardoning iniquity
And passing over the transgression of the remnant of His heritage?
He does not retain His anger forever,
Because He delights in mercy.
He will again have compassion on us,
And will subdue our iniquities.
You will cast all our sins
Into the depths of the sea.
—Micah 7:18-19

8

A New Store, House, and Land

By 1938, Daddy had saved a little money in the store business. Across the road from the store was about a hundred acres of land that was for sale. This land had been repossessed by the Federal Land Bank.

Daddy went to the bank to get more information about buying this land. He wanted to know how much a down payment would be, and how many years he would have to pay for it. They were asking $1,200 for the 100 acres.

The purchase was made, and it was not long until Daddy was building our new home across the road from where we lived in the store. It was wonderful to have several rooms in the house, new furniture, and a comfortable place to live. In a year or so, he built a new store near our house. These were exciting days. He also built a barn for the horses and cows, and a chicken house.

We had always had a bored well, and sometimes we would almost run out of water. We now had a dug well with plenty of water. It was dug by hand. One person would go down in the well to dig out the dirt, while another person pulled the dirt out by five-gallon buckets. They dug until they struck water. A round wooden curb was made and dropped into the well, which shielded the water from being in contact with the dirt wall. There was still dirt at the top of the well. Dad then built a cover above ground to keep anything from getting in it, and to also house the pulley and water bucket.

One day while they were digging deep in the well, I asked Daddy to let me go down in the bucket. He put me in it, and down I went, all the way to the bottom of the well. When I looked up all I could see was a round hole and the sky above. That was fun, but I don't think Mother approved of that when she found out about it.

Another day I will never forget was the day we got electricity in the store and house. We got a refrigerator, and now we could have ice anytime we wanted it and cold milk. Mother made us ice cream in the ice trays. We soon got an electric radio and would listen to the Grand Ole Opry every Saturday night. Sometimes we would have several neighbors come, since they didn't have a radio. If we had the radio on and heard the President's voice, everyone in the house rushed to hear what he was saying. Franklin Delano Roosevelt was President from 1933 to 1945, so it was easy to recognize his voice.

We also got a telephone, which was called a party line. If someone was talking on the phone, we had to wait until they hung up before we could make our call. Everyone on the line had a special ring, such as a long and a short ring, or two short rings. If we wanted to talk with someone in town or on another line, we had to ring one time to get the operator and tell her who we wanted to talk with.

We had a gas tank put in at our store, so we now sold a lot of gasoline. I remember selling it for about 11 to 19 cents a gallon. Some people only bought a gallon or two, because it was still hard times. The gas was pumped by a handle to a ten-gallon glass storage tank, where the marks on the tank would indicate how many gallons were sold.

Now we had plenty of land to raise all the vegetables we needed, and even some to sell. We had big patches of corn, potatoes, cucumbers, okra, peas, and peanuts. There was a large pasture for

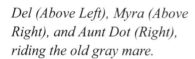

Del (Above Left), Myra (Above Right), and Aunt Dot (Right), riding the old gray mare.

the cows and horses. We had a gray mare that we liked to ride and we would sing, "The old gray mare, she ain't what she used to be."

Soon after World War II started, there were several things that were rationed, one of which was sugar. Also in Mississippi, tokens were used in paying sales tax. There was a silver-colored and a gold-colored token. The tokens were hard to deal with when it came to sales transactions. Everything was going well in the store until one day the Mississippi Sales Tax people came to see Daddy. They had their books with them that showed how much he had sold and how much he owed. He told them he knew he had paid on every penny that he had sold. Finally, the problem was solved. If

I remember correctly, they told him he was supposed to pay tax on all the food and items we had taken from the store for family use. Paying sales tax was something new to his small business. He was accurate in his sales tax, but not aware of items used by the family. It took several months to pay the money he owed in these hard times with his meager income.

Yes, there were taxes, but the government asked for other things at this time too, such as scrap metal. As I have mentioned, there was no garbage. Everything was used. Scrap iron and rubber were two items that people gathered from their surroundings and sold or donated during World War II.

A Nickel's Worth of Cheese and Crackers

Daddy didn't like to raise the price of goods, but he had to do so in order to make ends meet. When he had to pay more for

the goods, his prices had to be raised. One day one of his regular customers came in and said, "I want a nickel's worth of cheese and crackers."

The cheese had made a steep price jump the day before. Daddy took a lunch sack, put in a few crackers and held the big hoop of cheese up to this fellow's nose. He closed the sack and reached for the nickel.

The fellow looked at Daddy with a big grin on his face and said, "Where's the cheese?"

Daddy said, "Oh, the cheese is so high today that all you get for a nickel is a good smell of it."

Of course, he was only kidding. The man left laughing, with his slice of hoop cheese and crackers, along with an RC Cola and Moon Pie for his lunch.

One day another man came in the store and told Daddy he wanted a bottle of "Rab Ber." After a lot of discussion with this man, Daddy finally found out that what he wanted was a bottle of "Brer Rabbit" molasses. I guess this was harder to figure out than the person who came in one country store asking for some goose tape. He really wanted duck tape!

The school bus drivers had a wonderful place at the store to sit around the potbelly stove, tell tales, chew Brown's Mule tobacco, and dip Red Rooster snuff. My grandfather, who lived nearby, often came to sit and visit with them.

One day a salesman came by and brought some samples of Garrett Sweet Snuff for Daddy to let his customers try.

There was a big spittoon near the stove. Now I could imagine a lot of spitting going on with the new snuff and having a big clean-up job that night.

I was like my daddy when it came to playing jokes on people. I was helping in the store when I saw some quinine capsules on the shelf near the snuff. The thought came to me to empty a couple of these capsules in the sample box of sweet snuff. For those of you who do not know about quinine, it is extremely bitter. I thought this might cure the school bus drivers of dipping and spitting on the floor, as they missed the spittoon. I could envision one getting the box and passing it around.

This didn't happen. Late that afternoon, low and behold, it was my grandfather who reached for the new sample box of sweet snuff, pulled his lower lip down, filled it full, and went out the backdoor on his way to the barn. About halfway there, he went into a fit, spitting, coughing, and made his way to the well that was nearby.

The next day when the bus drivers came to the store, my grandfather looked at my daddy and them and said, "I want to tell ya'll something. If all that W. E. Garrett Snuff is like that—W. E. can have it all back, it's bitter as quinine!"

I made my getaway fast, because I was about to explode, holding back the laughter. I looked at Daddy as I left. I knew *he*

knew exactly what had happened.

My husband, Russ, remembers a story similar to this. A man often sat around in a local drugstore in the small town of Water Valley. This gentleman left the drugstore, went across the street, and sat down on a park bench. He put his head back and went sound asleep. One of his friends who was still in the drugstore at the time said, "I believe I'll have some fun."

He got some quinine, quietly walked over to the park bench, poured some of the bitter liquid into the man's gaping mouth, and hurried back to the drugstore. Everyone waited to see what would happen. In a very short time the man on the bench jumped straight up and came running across the street to the drugstore. He yelled in a loud voice, "Give me something quick; I think my gall has done busted!"

These were good days. Stories were shared, and we had laughter along with our hard work. We had a comfortable place to live and the store business was getting better. We continued to enjoy living close to the school and church. We had good friends and family living near us. The Lord had blessed us in many ways.

Great is the LORD, and greatly to be praised; ...
—Psalm 145:3

9

A Mockingbird Sang in a Sweet Gum Tree

Daniel, a black preacher, came to our store often. He and Daddy would laugh and talk for a long time when he came for his nickel's worth of coal oil (kerosene). The can always had a crisp potato stuck on the spout. Sometimes he brought a glass jug with a cap on it. He often told interesting stories that I would hear when I was at the store.

One day I told him about the mockingbird that was singing at night in the sweet gum tree in our front yard. It was keeping Mother awake. I didn't want anything to bother my mother. No one, I don't think, could have loved their mother any more than I did mine. Sometimes Daddy would get up in the night and throw a stick of stove wood into the tree to quiet it for a while. If Daddy was asleep, I would sometimes get up and scare it from the tree myself. This bird, with its various sounds and incessant singing, bothered me because it bothered Mother.

Daniel listened as I told my story. He said he had always heard if a mockingbird sang for three nights in your yard, that someone there was going to die.

My folks had taught us not to be superstitious about things like going under a ladder, a black cat crossing the road in front of your car, rocking a rocking chair with no one in it, and other things that people said were bad luck. I didn't believe this about the mockingbird, but I couldn't seem to get it off my mind. I was determined, however, to get rid of this bird. I had been told that it was the state bird, and you didn't shoot or kill a state bird.

One night it seemed to me that the mockingbird sang the entire night. The next morning, I had a plan. I waited for Daddy to leave for Memphis, taking a load of peas to sell. I got the rifle and went mockingbird hunting. I was a good shot, as Daddy had taught me to shoot the rifle years before. He put Coke caps in a dirt bank across the road, and I would practice shooting them. He would throw bad apples or empty snuff boxes as high as he could, and I would shoot them coming down. I often went squirrel hunting with him and brought home one or two. Mother made wonderful squirrel stew and dumplings for us to eat. On this particular morning, however, I

was not hunting for food, but I was focused on one thing. I put my plan into action.

I heard the mockingbird and saw it perched in a tall pine tree across the road. I put the gun barrel against a post at the store and got a good view of my target. I pulled the trigger and down came the bird. As I went across the road to look at it, I saw Daddy's truck at a neighbor's house, where he was picking up some peas. I knew he could have heard the shot. He was a great Daddy, he knew my heart, and that I did it for my mother. He didn't reprimand me. He could be firm with us and we knew to mind him. If we got out of line, he would threaten us with his leather strap, but in this case no punishment ever came. To kill this mockingbird was a blessing to me, just knowing that my mother could sleep soundly again, and this made me sleep soundly too.

I never told anyone about shooting the mockingbird, not even Daniel. Some things are better left unsaid. He came to the store often, but we never talked about the mockingbird again.

In that day I will make a covenant for them
With the beasts of the field,
With the birds of the air,
And with the creeping things of the ground.
Bow and sword of battle I will shatter from the earth,
To make them lie down safely.
—Hosea 2:18

10

Baptizing in the O'Tuckolofa Creek

I am so grateful for Christian parents who set the example and led me to know Christ through the home and church. Also there were wonderful grandparents before them who put Christ first in their lives. Our family was always at church when we had

O'Tuckolofa Church members.

a worship service. I remember going with my grandmother on Saturday afternoon to put flowers in the church and sweep or clean the sanctuary.

Every year in August, we had a revival meeting. It usually lasted a week, with morning and evening services. Sometimes it would only be at night, according to how much work the farmers still had to do. A visiting preacher would be invited to preach the revival. Day or night, it would be very warm in the church. At night with the windows up, all kinds of bugs came in, and I remember having to fight them.

Baby Del with her mother and family members.

Mother always tried to bring comfort to her little girls. She would fill a vanilla flavoring bottle with water and put it in her purse, so she could give us a swallow of water if we got thirsty. She also included a few crackers, if we got restless. Most of my early life we lived near enough to walk to the church. Many times I would go to sleep in Mother's arms, and Daddy would carry me home asleep and put me to bed. The next morning I would wake up in my bed, without any recollection of leaving church and coming home.

It was at one of these August revivals that Myra, age nine, went down the aisle to tell the preacher that she had accepted Christ as her Savior, and she wanted to join the church and be baptized. There had been much discussion before this day. Our parents wanted to be sure this was her own decision and not because a friend was joining.

She was very sure, and afterwards, she started working on me. She preached to me, read to me, and advised me as to what I needed to do. At my age, I didn't understand it all. The baptismal service was planned and set for a Sunday in August. There were several to be baptized. Some of the men from the church went down to the creek and cut bushes and cleared the grass where the people would be standing. The water could not be too deep, because there were some small children to be baptized.

Everyone had to walk from the church to this place, because there was no road, not even a wagon road. Mother took a little raincoat to put around Myra after she was baptized. The preacher went down into the water, which was somewhat muddy, and you couldn't see under the water. I hoped there was no "sinking sand" under it. I had heard about this kind of sand. I was always afraid of snakes, and I had often seen snakes in this creek. Also whenever I got into grass or the woods, I always got covered in chiggers or red bugs as I called them.

Several people went down into the water before Myra. When she went down, I surely hoped all the snakes had been scared away. She was baptized, as the rest had been, in the Name of the Father,

Group waiting to be baptized.

*Baptizing in the
O'Tuckolofa Creek.*

the Son, and the Holy Ghost, and she came up without any problem and walked out. Mother put the little raincoat around her as others went down into the water. A few minutes later, Myra fell down on the ground. She fainted out cold, as I stood looking on, scared to death. I thought my sister had died.

She was given attention by several people. They took the coat off, fanned her, put water on her face, and she soon came to life in a short time. I can't remember anything about the rest of the day. But one thing that stuck in my mind for a long time was that I knew I didn't want to be baptized in the O'Tuckolofa Creek.

As the years passed there were more baptisms, more revivals, two singing schools, and all day singings with dinner on the ground. By this time we had built outside tables that were used when we had all-day meetings. There was a pump that had to be primed each time we wanted to get water, so we always kept a bucket or bottle of water near the pump.

Also, occasionally, a group would come to the church to teach piano lessons. They would teach individual lessons for two weeks. Myra went to all the lessons and learned to play the piano pretty well. I went one time at the insistence of my parents and it was awful. I didn't want to sit and try to learn something I didn't like. I would rather be outside playing or working. About this time I saved up enough money to buy a guitar for a little over three dollars. I learned to play some songs by just using the instruction book.

Soon after we would have a revival, when I was about six to eight years old, I often preached in the backyard to any creature that was there. I tried to remember what the preacher had preached, and I would get on a tree stump and let the live creatures out there have it! I did this when my family was not around.

I will never forget the times when the school would turn out to let the children walk down to the church during a morning revival service. An invitation was given and a little second-grade boy came down the aisle and joined the church. I told my parents about his decision, and I wondered if he knew what he was doing. Anyway, he came to church after that when he could. It was a long way to walk, but he did walk to church when he couldn't get a ride. Through the years I was in school with him. As I watched the life of this young boy, I observed him in school, and heard how he went on in his studies to become a preacher and a schoolteacher for the rest of his life. He was pastor of the O'Tuckolofa Church for a short time.

I cannot help but think back on the many blessings of this country church. My immediate family and extended family were well represented in the membership. This was home. It was peace and security. I was glad Myra survived her baptism, but I did not have to worry about sinking sand or snakes or red bugs or any creek-related fears for myself, because I was not baptized in the O'Tuckolofa! This creek that ran behind our church was not a shining river, nor did it have a crystal tide; but my family was there,

all gathered together, and I knew that God was there, and my heart
was happy …

> Soon we'll reach the shining river,
> Soon our pilgrimage will cease,
>
> Soon our happy hearts will quiver
> with the melody of peace.
>
> Yes, we'll gather at the river,
> the beautiful, the beautiful river;
>
> Gather with the saints at the river
> that flows by the throne of God.

****

*Therefore, if anyone is in Christ, he is a new creation; old
things have passed away; behold, all things have become new.*

—2 Corinthians 5:17

11

Tornado
March 16, 1942

I was thirteen years old, and it was Friday, the thirteenth. This day ended a happy week of school for me, but when Monday, March 16, 1942 arrived, it was a day I will never forget.

I doubt if there was another teenager who enjoyed life more than I did, at school, at home, playing, and working on our 100-acre farm at O'Tuckolofa.

A school, church, many homes, farms, and our country store

were within the radius of this small community.

Sunday, March 15, was a very warm, sunny day. I remember we were walking to church, when Mother stopped and said, "I need to go back to the house and change clothes; I'm dressed too warm." We waited for her before going on to church. The principal of the school came in the church about the same time we did. He taught the adult Sunday School Bible lesson.

The Barber Family right before the tornado.

The next day, Monday, was cloudy and extremely windy. It was very warm. The day went by about as usual, playing softball at recess, and having our regular schoolwork. That afternoon, the eighth grade practiced their play for the end of school. I had one of the leading parts. My aunt, Dorothy, was one of my eighth-grade teachers and was directing the play.

Somehow, there was sort of a depressed feeling as we sat in study hall waiting for the bell to ring. A lady who lived about a mile down the road came rushing in; all eyes turned to her, as she said in a very stressful tone of voice, "I've come to get my child—it's coming the worst cloud I've ever seen, back in the west."

She and her little girl left in a hurry, walking home. Our school had only eight grades. The high school students rode a bus to another school. The bus had not come to pick up the O'Tuckolofa students. The principal came in and told all the students who usually walked home to leave early before it started raining.

As I walked home, I also noticed a very dark cloud in the west, and it was already thundering. I hurried on to our store where I knew my parents would be. They were very emotional about the approaching cloud.

My parents, grandparents, and Daniel were in the store when I got there. My Aunt Dorothy soon came. Daddy ran to the barn to let the horses out. He thought they would be safer out of the barn than in it. Mother was standing at the front door watching for the bus to bring Myra from another school. She soon got home and now we were all together in the store. The store was below the house, so we always thought it would be safer than the house on the hill. The cloud was very dark, almost black-green in color, and the lightning was frightening and continuous. There was a constant rumble of thunder.

Daniel, the black preacher, had come to the store for a nickel, or maybe a dime's worth, of coal oil because he had a gallon glass jug that day. I was glad the mockingbird topic never came up. He got his jug and was about ready to leave. Daddy told him that the cloud was too close for him to leave and be caught out in it walking home. Daniel put his jug down and decided to stay.

Our family of seven and Daniel were sitting around in different places, on sacks of feed, nail kegs, the ice box, and in a chair or two. Prayers were being said by everyone, as we looked out the window, seeing things going through the air. We were praying for protection, for we all knew this was the worst time of our life.

Daddy was standing up looking out the window, and he hollered to us to get on the floor. Within seconds, the sky came down on us and it became dark as night. The last thing I saw was the west wall beginning to lean in our direction. We all fell to the floor as the darkness surrounded us. We could not hear, see, or even think what was happening. Minutes later, the rain and hail beat upon us in such torrents that it was almost unbearable. Somehow an old tarpaulin from the old store had blown near us; Daddy found it and put it over most of us, as there was no roof over us.

As the storm began to calm down, our family was bleeding, bruised, and had broken bones. We were on the floor in a mass of debris. There were several gallons of sorghum molasses spilled on the floor, along with shoe polish, broken bottles, groceries, and all the other things that were in the store. Everyone was moving around in this stuff, trying to get up and check on each other. Daniel was not moving, and near him were the store scales. They were big and heavy and may have fallen on him, causing his death.

Amidst the rain and suffering, I looked in the direction of the school and teachers' home. There was no house and no school. I saw the principal's wife clutching one of her twin baby girls as she called for Edwin, her husband. I learned later that they were sitting side by side, each holding one of their six-month-old twins. Then I looked in the direction of our church, and there was nothing left that one could recognize as being a place of worship. Little was left of our house, store, and other buildings on our farm. The basketball goalpost, some steps, and a few scattered bricks were all

Basketball goalpost and school steps after the tornado.

that survived of the school.

Later my sister found only one note of her piano, which she was so proud of and was learning to play. About the only thing in the house that was left was my bicycle. My bicycle was found near the house with a quilt wrapped around it.

My Aunt Dorothy made her way up to the teachers' home to help the principal's wife look for her husband, Edwin, and the other baby. She did find them, but not alive. Their car was demolished.

The LORD has His way
In the whirlwind and in the storm,
And the clouds are the dust of His feet.
—Nahum 1:3

Feebly, we made our way to a neighbor's house as soon as we could after it stopped raining. I almost didn't make it. I remember sitting down in the mud and grass several times along the way. Myra had only minor injuries and was trying to help me and keep me going. She kept saying, "Come on, Del; come on, Del; you can make it!"

The wonderful neighbors, whose house was not damaged, helped us get on some dry clothes. They put a pair of overalls on Daddy, and when he got to the hospital he couldn't believe he was wearing overalls, because he didn't have any of his own. One in our group had on some part of a Santa Claus suit.

Trees had to be cut out of the road for miles before the ambulance and transportation could take us the five miles to the Water Valley Hospital and temporary first aid places. I remember hearing someone say they were taking me on to Baptist Hospital in Memphis, and Dorothy was going with me. I don't remember going to the hospital or anything for many days. Myra stayed to help with Mother, Daddy, and my grandparents.

I Thought I Was Now In Heaven

After several days in the hospital, I regained consciousness and looked around in this very unfamiliar place. I didn't see anyone at the time. I got up and went to the window and looked out. All I saw was blue sky and a few white fluffy clouds. Then I looked down and saw tiny cars and people moving around. They were so little and looked so far away from my vantage point. I looked down at the white clothes I was wearing. I had never worn clothes that looked like this. I turned and looked at the room and a door going into a hallway. I saw someone else dressed in white clothes in the hall. She had something white on her head, and I thought it was some sort of crown. With all these images before me *I thought that I was now in Heaven.* Yes, something must have happened, and I had died and gone to Heaven. I moved beyond my room and saw other people dressed in white with crowns on their heads. These most assuredly would be angels, since I knew I was above the earth when I looked out the window. I stood in amazement, admiring them.

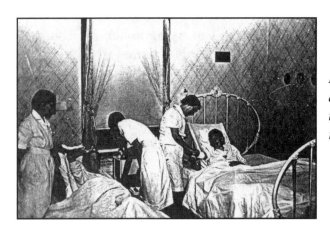

Hospital beds and nurses tending the injured.

All at once one of these angels caught me by the arm and ushered me right back into the room and put me in the bed. She pulled up some bars all around my bed. It was at this time I didn't think so highly of these so-called angels. I thought for sure that she had put me in jail! This angel talked rather sternly to me and told me not to get out of bed again. That's not all she did—she hooked me up to something with a hissing sound and put it in my nose. By now I thought I might even be in the gas chamber. I asked her a few questions, but the answers did not make sense. She patted my arm and left.

After a short time Aunt Dorothy came in, consoled me, and began telling me some of the things that had happened and where I was.

To a thirteen-year-old who had never been sick or away from home for any length of time, the days in the hospital passed slowly. As I got better I was distressed as I tried to remember what had happened. Like a jigsaw puzzle, I began to try to put together the pieces of a heavenly experience that was now a nightmare and had become a reality. My aunt brought me games and things to occupy my time. She told me I had been in a tornado and hurt seriously, with a punctured lung, broken collarbone, cuts and bruises, and losing a lot of blood. I was told by a few friends, who had family members in the hospital, that my folks were doing all right. This was strange, because I knew if they were not hurt they would come to the hospital to see about me.

Jesus was my Savior. I had asked Him into my heart and life, but I had not made a profession of my faith before the church. I knew that I should go before the church with this decision. I knew how to pray. I prayed and asked the Lord to let me get well, go home, and find my loved ones alive and well. I made a promise that day that I would serve Him and tell others about Jesus Christ all the days of my life.

I returned to my loved ones to find them also trying to recover from physical problems; however, this day was an answer to my prayers, and I was filled with overwhelming joy. The days to follow were filled with many problems during my convalescence—more days in the hospital, getting a house where we could be together, clothes, and the necessities of life. We had no material things and no money. We did have the best of friends and family, and an awesome God who supplied our needs. The help from American Red Cross will never be forgotten. They supplied so many of our needs.

When I was able, I went to O'Tuckolofa to see where I had lived and enjoyed so many of my childhood days. There was no country store where Daddy would sell cheese and crackers, bologna, RC Colas, Moon Pies, coal oil, W. E. Garrett Snuff, and Brown Mule chewing tobacco. Mother wouldn't have to be concerned about selling on the credit or opening the store on Sunday. There was no school or church. There would be no more all-day singings or revivals and baptizing in the O'Tuckolofa Creek. All of this went through my mind.

Many of our friends and neighbors also lost their homes. There were fifteen killed and many injured in our community and county.

I thought about Daniel and the mockingbird that sang at midnight in the sweet gum tree. He was the only one who died that day in our store. There in front of where the store had been, I saw Daniel's gallon glass jug of coal oil on the ground, unbroken.

The site where the store stood.
Note the coal oil jug unbroken in the foreground.

As I looked at that jug I thought—this was to be used to light his lamp, but on March 16, he exchanged this earthly coal oil lamp light for the eternal light of his Lord and Savior, Jesus Christ.

I looked toward the school, and all I could see were the steps and the goalpost in front of where the school had been. There I had played basketball and tennis many times. In my journal, written long ago, was a four-line poem I wrote remembering those days:

Will your goalpost stand,
when the storms of life are out of hand?
Anchored in Christ's love and care,
we can look beyond the clouds we bear.

****

Your mercy, O LORD, is in the heavens;
Your faithfulness reaches to the clouds.
                                              —Psalm 36:5

12

After the Tornado

New store with Del's mother, Myra, and PaPa Harvey in the background.

Many people who saw Daddy after the tornado would ask him, "What are you going to do now?"

Dad told them, "Just build back as soon as I can. When you are down and you don't know what to do, you just have to look up— especially for the Lord's directions." He had the land, but it was not completely paid for. We had no money, food, clothes, house, or necessities of life. The Red Cross gave us some money, and family and friends let us live with them for a while. Other people gave us clothes and some useful items. Even used bath cloths and sheets were appreciated.

Daddy got a very bad injury on his leg during the tornado and had to use crutches for several weeks. When he was walking a little better that summer, he began to make plans to rebuild the house on the same spot as the one that blew away.

The house was finished that summer, and it was a happy day when we were all together in our own home. Friends and relatives had been a great help to accomplish this. The money we received from the Red Cross helped to buy some much-needed furniture.

It was sad, however, to look around us to see all the debris from the storm. The school, teachers' home, church, and our dear neighbors were all gone. Dad soon decided he had to rebuild the store in order to have an income. He hoped there would be enough people from surrounding communities to support his business.

Church members and neighbors started rebuilding the church. Daddy helped on it when he could, even though he was still on crutches. One day I was able to go to the church and saw Daddy laying bricks on the foundation. I asked him if I could put one brick in place. He handed me the trowel. I put some mortar on it, put it in place, tapped it down, and scraped off the excess mortar as I had seen him do it. I wanted to have a tiny part in laying the foundation of the new O'Tuckolofa church. The church had been very instrumental in forming the foundation of my life. It meant so much to me as a child and also to my family; in fact, there have been 19 of my family who have been members of the O'Tuckolofa Church through the years.

In September 1942, the first service was held in the new church. It was not long after this that a revival was held and many people made professions of faith. I was one of those. I could not forget the commitment I had made to the Lord as I was recuperating in the Baptist Hospital in Memphis after the tornado. I began to wonder where we would be baptized, as it was October and too cold to go to the O'Tuckolofa Creek. The pastor got permission to use the baptistery at First Baptist Church in Water Valley. This pleased me very much, as I still couldn't forget the day Myra fainted on the banks of the O'Tuckolofa Creek after she was baptized.

When we were settled in our new house, Daddy built the store and a barn for the livestock and storage needs. Daddy soon stocked the store and was back in business.

Mother was very unhappy and lonesome as she missed her friends and neighbors. Also her mother, daddy, and sister who lived on our land before the tornado decided not to move back. Myra and I rode a school bus to Water Valley now, and we could not walk to school or come home for lunch, as had been our custom before the tornado.

Myra was in the eleventh grade and I was in the ninth grade. I had missed several weeks of school after the tornado, but they let me start that year in the ninth grade with my classmates. I was enjoying being in a new school except for one thing. I couldn't see very well. Even though I sat on the front row, I still couldn't read what was written on the board. I knew I was nearsighted at an early age. When I was in about the second grade, some people came to the school to check our vision. The big chart was put up and we all got in a line. When it came my time I couldn't read the letters, so my best friend standing behind me whispered to me what they were. I probably could have gotten free glasses at that time. I knew I shouldn't have done that, but I was afraid they would think I was dumb and couldn't read. As I got older I kept telling my daddy I couldn't see like everyone else, and I needed glasses. He was reluctant and always said he hated to see me have to wear glasses so young.

Anyway, the year I was in the ninth grade, I got my first pair of glasses. That was a wonderful day. I could now see the birds, leaves on the trees, and the blackboard at school. It had been embarrassing to have to walk up close to the board and copy my algebra questions. Then one day when we were getting off the bus, a boy's elbow landed in my face, breaking my glasses. I hated to tell my parents when I got home that day. They were still short of money, but they managed to get a new lens for my glasses.

Daddy and Mother often talked about selling the house, store, and land and moving to town. They knew it would be better for us. There would be more opportunities, and we would be near the school.

Word got out that Daddy was willing to sell his property. One day a man came by and made him an offer to buy it. He got enough money to pay off the land debt and buy a house in Water Valley. Now there was the task of finding a job.

Dad, for a few years, worked in other people's grocery stores. He rented buildings and was in business again. He soon built his own store.

A few years later, he was city marshal for seven years and then elected sheriff of Yalobusha County. Mother got a job as a seamstress when we were in high school and college, which helped us financially. I got a job on Saturdays working in a grocery store for $2.00 a day. I was thrilled to have this job, but was a little disappointed when I got paid that first Saturday. It was only $1.98. I learned that the two cents was taken out for tax.

The theater was just across the street from the store where I worked. It cost ten cents to see a movie. It was crowded on Saturday as folks came to town to see their favorite cowboy movie. In the 1940s, life was much different from what it is today.

This time in the 1940s, World War II took young boys from high school and college to be in service. I can remember one of my friends named Dixie had an older brother. When we were younger, Myra and I spent many fun hours playing over at Dixie's house. It was a sad day when we found out that "Red," Dixie's brother, had been killed in the war. When I completed the eleventh grade, I went to summer school, which permitted me to start to college in the fall. I was sixteen years old when I joined my sister, Myra, at Northwest Community College in Senatobia. It was her second year there. I got a job washing glasses in the cafeteria that paid ten dollars a month. One day my English Literature teacher asked me to start grading papers for her. I needed the money, but I didn't want to put grades on the papers. I reluctantly took the job. After two years at Northwest and summer school at Ole Miss, Myra and I both got teaching jobs. We needed the money in order to get our college degrees. God blessed us in many ways during these years.

Trust in the LORD with all your heart,
And lean not on your own understanding;
In all your ways acknowledge Him,
And He shall direct your paths.
                    —Proverbs 3:5-6

13

Del and Russ

Myra and I were at Northwest Community College one year together. We were on our way home on a bus one weekend. The bus would stop several times between Senatobia and Water Valley. The cost was a little over three dollars for this trip. Daddy gave us $30.00 a month. We had to pay a $22.00 fee to the college, which left us $8.00 to spend for any needs we had. We always went home once a month, so that left us enough money to buy a hamburger, go to a movie, or walk downtown for a needed item.

The bus stopped at Sardis, Mississippi, and we went in the station. One of our classmates was also on the bus going to her home. We saw her

Del and Russ on their wedding day, July 10, 1954.

talking to a boy dressed in a navy uniform. She motioned for us to come over where she was. She said, "I want you to meet Russell Edward Aven, one of my high school classmates from Water Valley."

We learned he had been traveling on a train from California. Our classmate talked about him on our way home. She told us how smart he was, and emphasized over and over how handsome he was. This was in 1945. It was not until five years later that our paths crossed again.

Russ in his Navy uniform.

A teacher friend of mine, Lib, and I were downtown in Water Valley, and we decided to go in a clothing store. Lib wanted to look for a suit. It was here that we were introduced to Russell Edward by his Aunt Frances, who was the clerk. Lib looked at the clothes and was soon ready to leave, when Aunt Frances looked at her nephew and said, "Russell Edward, why don't you take Del and Lib to Turnage Drug Store for a sundae?" Since he didn't have a girlfriend and was rather shy, she must have thought this would be a good time to get him a girlfriend.

We three left for the drugstore and enjoyed a sundae as we chatted a while—mostly Lib and me. When we got ready to leave, he politely said, "May I drive you home?"

I said, "Thank you, but I'll just walk across the street to my dad's store." Lib agreed to be driven home.

I asked Lib the next day how everything went the rest of the afternoon. She said he drove her straight home. She thanked him, and they both said good-bye, and she got out of the car. That was it.

In the summer of 1950, I was commuting to Ole Miss with different people because I didn't have a car. Russ saw me one day and told me if I ever needed a ride to Ole Miss to let him know, because he was driving up there each day also. This was much better than the way I was going, because he could pick me up at my house and bring me back home in the afternoon. From this time forth, there were several rook parties, tennis games, movies, and of course, commuting to Ole Miss.

By May of 1951, Russ had finished his degrees in Chemical Engineering and Mathematics, and was hired by Oak Ridge National Laboratories, in Oak Ridge, Tennessee. Between us there were many letters written, and probably thousands of miles driven between Oak Ridge and Water Valley, during the next three years.

A wedding was soon planned for July 10, 1954, and as I write this, we have had sixty wonderful years together.

After two years in Oak Ridge, Russ got a teaching position at Ole Miss. We moved to Oxford with our precious little curly-headed girl, Debra. In 1960, the Lord blessed us again with our precious little boy, Anson.

Family photos of Del, Russ, Anson, and Debra.

We had the joy and privilege of having them at home until they finished college and then some.

Russ retired after teaching 40 years at Ole Miss. On July 10, 2004 we celebrated our fiftieth wedding anniversary. That was ten years ago!

Fiftieth wedding anniversary celebration.

14

"High Sheriff"
The Life of a Sheriff in
the 1960s

My daddy, Forest Barber, had been a farmer, country store owner, city store owner, city police officer, and had various jobs through the years. He was elected sheriff and spent three years and nine months in a constant struggle to keep his county peaceful, crushing the forces of evil, and enduring the maladies of his physical body.

The sheriff-elect died a month before he was to take office. People wasted no time asking the long-time, well-liked city policeman Barber to run for the office.

Forest, with his sheriff's cap and gun.

He had been defeated in a county supervisor race before, and he was not sure he was ready for the cynicism that always accompanies this kind of political race. There would be wearing away of shoe leather, knocking on doors, maybe some dog bites, and the high cost of the campaign. He was told during the last race he was in, "There are cow ticks, dog ticks, and deer ticks, but worse than these is *politics*!"

With much encouragement, he entered the race. The race was run and the day of the election was the first day of March. Even nature seemed to be against him on this morning. As he looked outside he saw a very freakish phenomenon for March in Mississippi. The ground was covered in snow and the snow was still falling. He was afraid that his supporters would not come to vote in a special election on such a snowy day. But they did come! Chains clicked up and down the streets, bringing in voters, along with country mud.

Forest Barber was in the run-off. This meant two more long weeks, subjected to the whims and avidity of his friends and the derision of his opponents.

On April 16, my dad took over the duties of sheriff and tax collector of Yalobusha County. By taking this office in April, he received little money for his first year's work, after his deputies and office help were paid. He had missed the January tax money; a percentage of which would have been his main salary.

People knocked on his door at all hours, and rarely a night passed without several telephone calls. He took no vacation time, and weekends found him busier than ever. However, each Sunday he was found in church, if at all possible, and rarely did anyone call him from his pew.

He spent some of his time collecting tax money, opening court, or delivering subpoenas. Most of his time was spent dealing with the lawbreakers and the evils of the county. It may seem strange in today's world, what will be said about alcohol in the following pages, but at this time it was illegal to sell whiskey or beer in Yalobusha County. Of course, wildcat/moonshine whiskey was unlawful.

Two Boys Happy to be Arrested

On cold, snowy, or rainy nights, there seemed to be more trouble. It was on one of these snowy nights, when the thermometer continued to drop and the piercing winds blew, that he thought surely no one would be out causing trouble. The sheriff was off to bed early. The inevitable happened. The phone rang.

The call was from the far corner of the county. He deputized two policemen to ride with him. A small country store had been broken into, and the marauders were being held at gunpoint outside the store by the owner. When the sheriff arrived, he asked the owner where the two men were.

"There they are—right there," the store owner said, pointing to a heap of snow that appeared to be a small pile of wood.

The sheriff's flashlight cast a dim spot on the snow-lit ground. He looked at the man and back to the mound in disbelieving glances. He walked nearer, kicking into it, and out came the two young boys, armed only with pocket knives, shivering and shaking the snow from their bodies.

On recognizing the sheriff, one said, "Mr. Barber, you don't know how glad we are to see you. We are about to freeze to death."

They were more than ready for a warm ride to jail after their long wait in the falling snow. This was one of the easy arrests—very few were this easy.

Elevator Escape

To the black people of Yalobusha County, he was their friend, but they knew he meant what he said. He was the "High Sheriff" to them. Many a Saturday night he spent transporting them to the doctor or hospital, bleeding from knife-fighting brawls. Very few of them tried to escape during an arrest or from jail, because they knew their high sheriff would find them and bring them back to their original destination.

One did try a very unique escape one day. A small, crude elevator was used by the cook downstairs in the jail, to send food upstairs and come back down with the dirty dishes. It was operated by a windlass. A small young black boy was able to crawl inside and was lowered to the kitchen, when the lady cook needed to wash the dishes. She was expecting dishes—not what was dished out of the small elevator that day! The lady was so stunned that he had no trouble releasing his crumpled body from the small enclosure, and leaped to freedom through the back door.

Upon being notified, immediately the sheriff in the nearby courthouse caught sight of him, and the chase was on. It extended about half a mile up and down hills, around buildings, cars, trucks, and finally, he disappeared, like a rabbit in a hole. A few minutes later, the sheriff found him hiding inside a truck parked at the cotton gin.

"Come out of there!" demanded Barber.

"High Sheriff, you have run me to death," he panted.

Many men and boys were chased by the sheriff over the sagegrass patches or through the honeysuckle thickets of the county. For a fifty-eight-year-old man, he held his own among the younger set. Most of the pursued were caught, exhausted and ready to surrender.

Dad's Battle with Cancer

His second year in office found him fighting another battle— one for his life against cancer of the pharynx, near the base of his brain. It had spread to the glands in his neck and was inoperable. These were very trying days for our family.

He endured thirty days of cobalt treatments and the long days of after-effects. He no longer weighed 225 pounds, but 160 instead. Dad never missed a full day from his job because of his cancer. Every morning he or some of his friends would drive him to a Memphis hospital, about a hundred miles from his home in Water

Valley. He went for thirty days straight, and each afternoon or night he would be back on duty. This is not to say the going was easy—it wasn't. He was as determined to win this physical battle as he was the fight against the evils of his county.

A short time after he finished the thirty days of cobalt, the glands in his neck began to swell. He had to return to the hospital. The doctor implanted radium seeds permanently in his neck. After this, Dad's fine Christian doctor told him he had done all he knew to do for him, and the rest was in the hands of the Lord.

Daddy did not have any medical insurance, and he knew there would be large medical bills. As mentioned earlier, he received little pay for his first year in office. Mother was very concerned, but he comforted her by saying everything was going to turn out all right. Many prayers went up in his behalf.

Mother and Daddy both were strengthened by their strong faith in the Lord and His Word that says, "… My grace is sufficient for you, for My strength is made perfect in weakness" (2 Corinthians 12:9), and also, "… I will never leave you nor forsake you" (Hebrews 13:5).

Before he had completely recovered from the cobalt, a drunk

Forest and his wife, Ora Lee.

man caught him off-guard and shattered his damaged brittle cheek bone, split his lip, and knocked out some teeth. This was a man he knew very well, and Daddy had no thoughts that he would hit him. He apologized to Daddy many times, and wouldn't have done this at all, but alcohol made the difference in his thoughts and actions. It took Daddy several months to recover from this. He had more major surgeries in the years to come, unrelated to any of the above.

Later that year, Daddy did have a complete healing of the cancer. However, his salivary glands were damaged by the treatments. His mouth stayed dry, but he took a small bottle of water with him and took sips of water when he needed it.

His Work Continued

He carried a gun on occasion, but during the day he was often without one. He usually took a flat leather hand-made paddle, which he called a "slap-paddle." He never had to shoot his gun, and rarely, if ever, did he use it in making an arrest. There were times when he feared for his life against theirs.

One night a call came from the parents of a teenager. The boy was half-drunk and was threatening to kill them. They had made out papers for his arrest. The sheriff and deputies left their car on the road. Two deputies were to go to the back door and two to the front door. All was going well on this dark night until a neighbor heard the car stop. He turned on a very bright light, exposing the sheriff and one deputy plainly in the front yard. The teenager came out the front door with a double-barreled shotgun.

He shouted, "If you don't leave, I'll kill you." He gave more shouts, "I'm gonna' kill you!"

"Drop your gun, boy. You have only two shots and we have six each—two more men behind you. Don't you know you can't shoot us?" the sheriff yelled, as he walked closer to the porch where the boy was standing.

A few more words between them, and he dropped his gun and

was soon off to jail.

There were always drunks or maybe a shoplifter, bootlegger, family trouble, a wreck, stabbing, murder, or passing of a bad check to deal with. He made numerous trips to Whitfield with the mentally disturbed. There were, also, the dope addict and the drug peddler to cause more trouble.

One day Daddy was on his way to Whitfield, a mental institution, with two men, twins—one of which was to be admitted that day. They drove through a small town on their way, and Sheriff Barber saw his nephew on the street and he waved to him. He hollered and asked Daddy where he was going. Before Daddy had time to say anything, one of the men put his head out the window and hollered back to him, "Going crazy!"

The sheriff drove on as his nephew had his laugh for the day.

They got to Whitfield and went into the office to check in. When the officer asked which one was to be admitted, one of the men pointed to his brother and said, "He is."

The other brother perked up and said, pointing to the first, "No, he's the one!"

The other one said, "You're the one that's crazy, I'm not!"

This went on for a good while. Sheriff Barber had not been around them at all until that day. He told us later that they had a hard time finding out who was to stay there and who was to come back with him.

Many bootleggers and alcoholics had sad hearts as they drove past Sheriff Barber and his deputies, standing on the banks of the O'Tuckolofa River, dumping gallons of whiskey into it. On days that they saw this they were not singing, "Shall We Gather at the River?"

One day Barber was sitting at the table with his wife and children, a privilege he was usually denied. There came a loud knock at the door. It was a lady who lived down the street. She was out of breath and pleading, "Come, Mr. Barber, my husband is trying to kill me and the kids!"

Barber grabbed his slap-paddle and was down the street in no time.

She hollered to him, "You better not go in there, he'll kill you. He's drinking."

Barber opened the door and started inside, when the man came down on the sheriff's head with a stick of stove wood. This put a knot on his head and staggered him, almost knocking him down. When he got his footing, he came around with a slap-paddle haymaker that landed on the man's head. He fell to the floor, but had no serious damage. Barber rubbed his own head and felt the big knot. He soon got the man in his car and took him to jail. He was in and out of jail several times after this.

Ice Pick Encounter

Daddy had compassion for people. He did not like for anyone to suffer in any way. He could be seen shedding tears over situations he had encountered. He could also be seen taking food and clothes from his own home, or buying something to take to the destitute. Children had a very special place in his heart, for he had two of his own. He could never stand to see a black or white child mistreated. However, there were many who were shuffled between the law and their parents. Many trips were made to Columbia and Oakley, taking children who had committed crimes. Other children were taken from their parents and placed in foster homes.

A court order was given him to go into a rural community and pick up a child. The child was at home with her father. The mother rode in the car with the sheriff to get the child. He knocked on the door and out rushed the father with a rifle. The sheriff was able to get it without trouble. Sheriff Barber informed him he had orders to pick up the child and take her to the Child Welfare Office. The father shouted in a loud, stern voice, "I'll kill myself, if you take that child away."

The little girl was sent to the car. The sheriff told him he would be back in a short time with some papers to give him. The father shouted again, "Just send an ambulance on out here, for I'll be dead when you get back."

When Sheriff Barber arrived with the papers, the father of the child was stretched out on his back on the front porch, motionless. A neighbor had arrived a few minutes before and was standing on the ground beside the porch, as pale as the sheriff's ivory-colored car.

"Sheriff—he has about killed himself," he said.

"He's not dead, is he?" inquired the sheriff.

"Not yet, but he said he stuck an ice pick all the way through his heart," the neighbor said hurriedly. (My eight-year-old granddaughter was listening to this story one day and asked, "Grandmama, what is an ice pick?" For the younger generation— an ice pick was used to chip a block of ice. It had a wooden handle with a five or six-inch small, but long, metal pick with a sharp point on the end.)

Sheriff Barber's eyes scanned the porch for weapons and saw none; he bent down close and saw the man was breathing, but saw no blood.

"What a shame, I sure hate to see someone suffer like that. He's about gone. I really hate to see him suffering—hand me that ice pick over here. I'm going to put him out of his misery," said Barber.

The neighbor had little time to absorb what the sheriff had said, as the man's eyes flew open immediately, and he gave an open-mouthed yell, "Don't do it! Don't do it!" as he was scrambling to his feet.

Of course, there was no ice pick, and Daddy would never have done anything like this. He would have gotten help for him immediately if he thought the man was injured.

The sheriff's ploy and escapade left two stunned people behind, but he laughed all the way back to town. Jokes, pranks, or humorous tales told to a small group on the street were very much a part of his everyday life.

Fire

Almost before his laughter subsided, he received a call from a deputy to go with him to pick up a black man who was thought to be hiding in a small shack on 32 Highway.

Their knock on the door brought such a scramble inside that this small shack shook. There was loud talking and someone hollered, "It's the High Sheriff."

They pushed the door open and saw a blaze of fire reaching to the ceiling and the room filling with smoke. People were running, jumping, and trying to put out the fire. The sheriff and deputy began to help. After all calmed down, the sheriff asked, "What in the world happened?"

He learned they had been sitting around the stove drinking "Wildcat Whiskey," and when they saw the sheriff they got scared and dumped it into the stove, which caused an almost tragic blaze. I don't know if they found the boy they were looking for or not.

Ironing in Self-Defense

A woman was home ironing one day, when her drinking husband came in and decided to beat her up. The sheriff was called. In the meantime, she stuck the iron to his arms and hands as she tried to protect herself.

When the sheriff arrived, he asked, "Where is your husband now?"

"After I stuck that iron to the seat of his pants—the last I saw of him he was traveling on. What you gonna' do with me, Sheriff?" she asked.

"Nothing," said the sheriff, "and if he comes back drunk, beating you again—just give him another ironing out and call me!"

Finding the Whiskey

On another occasion Sheriff Barber was searching a place for whiskey. He saw a man and his dog. He told the man he had a search warrant to search for whiskey. The little dog came up to the sheriff and whined and switched his tail, then started down a trail through the woods. The dog would look back to see if the sheriff was following him. Barber followed the dog until the dog stopped at a spot in the woods. There, buried in the ground, was the whiskey. To this man, on this particular day, his dog didn't turn out to be his best friend.

Another man who was reported selling whiskey out of his home was Barber's next place to search. He went there more than once, but found nothing. Reports kept coming in. He hesitated to go out there again, because the man had told him about how sick his wife was. Anyway, he decided to go and do a more intensive search. He got his search warrant for the house and presented it to the man. He and his deputy began a search throughout the house. The man's wife was still bedridden. They said they were sorry to disturb her, but they had to search the entire house. They looked under her bed.

There was the whiskey! Many gallons and bottles of homemade whiskey were stored under her bed. After this disclosure the only person in this house that was really sick now was the man—not his wife, who was not sick at all!

Such were the days of one Mississippi sheriff. He was remembered by many as the "High Sheriff"—to others he was almost like a Santa Claus. He was praised by many, and probably cursed by some, but to me he was the best daddy a girl could have.

****

One night at church a young lad was sitting behind Daddy. He touched Daddy on the shoulder and said, "You know what I want to be when I grow up?"

"No, son, what is that?" Dad asked him.

"I want to grow up and be a sheriff just like you," he said very emphatically.

No better tribute could have been paid my daddy.

Sheriff memorabilia.

15

A Tribute to my Dad– Forest Barber
(Jan. 26, 1902–Dec. 30, 1987)

Written by Myra Barber (June 21, 1998 on Father's Day)

Forest beside the squad car.

Words cannot begin to say what my daddy contributed to my life. I hope many people can say the same thing about their dad.

Daddy, of course, had his faults, but he was a sinner saved by grace in his early manhood. He had a personal relationship with Jesus Christ. He loved his family so very much. He worked so hard to provide the necessities of life for his two daughters and his wife. He was a farmer, merchant, City Marshal of Water Valley, Mississippi and Sheriff of Yalobusha County, Mississippi. He treated everyone with fairness and gentleness. He tried to make a better person of the hardest criminals.

Daddy disciplined us with firmness. Most of the time we knew what he meant when he said, "Settle down." On a few occasions we did not, and Daddy threatened us with the razor strap. I cannot remember his ever using it on us, even though he may have come close when we forgot to bring in the firewood. Daddy always provided the best he could for his family. He did not have much of the world's goods, but he was rich in love, honesty, sincerity, faithfulness, encouragement, sympathy, and devotion.

He lived the right example before us. He may not have said, "I love you," as much as he should, but we knew he did by the things he provided for us. He was always willing to sacrifice for us. He never used profanity. I always knew he loved Mother dearly. My mother usually led the prayer time in our family, but Daddy said the blessing at the table most of the time.

When my mother and I were down, he always tried to cheer us. I remember one time in his life he had a cancerous inoperable tumor at the base of his brain. I was so depressed and disturbed. When the report came from the doctor, and my mother told him the news, he said, "I was expecting that, but everything will be all right." It was hard, but he came through it and lived many years.

Daddy was sympathetic with the poor. A few years ago, a lady told me when she was a child and didn't have money to buy pencils, she would bring eggs to the store and Daddy would buy them so she could have money for her pencils. Needless to say, she appreciated this favor on Dad's part.

Many tributes come from people like this person whom Daddy

treated with love and concern. As a policeman, Daddy helped schoolchildren cross the street to the school. They loved my daddy. Daddy trusted people, sometimes to his own downfall. Once Daddy was without any kind of protective weapon, and an intoxicated man hit him in the face and broke his jaw.

Most Saturday nights, Daddy was called to the block in Water Valley because of a stabbing. He was on call twenty-four hours a day. He put his total efforts into the task before him. While he was sheriff, as I said, he had cancer and had to take treatments of cobalt and radium seed. That was so hard, trying to carry on a job, and go to Memphis for a treatment. But he never gave up and the cancer was arrested.

One of the hardest experiences I ever had to go through with my Daddy was the last three years of his life. He became unable to swallow food or water, and had to have a gastrostomy and be fed through a tube in his stomach. Daddy loved to eat. Now he could not taste the food, but he could smell food cooking, and desired some of it so badly. It was so hard for me to eat around him, because I knew how much he wanted to eat home-cooked food. Never to taste food took away some of the pleasures of life.

Daddy was a good storyteller. He only had an eighth-grade education, but he could entertain people with his stories he told about real life.

When he was a merchant, it was very hard for him to refuse someone who needed groceries and did not have the money to purchase them. When he closed the grocery business, he had many accounts. Most of them were paid, but some were never paid. But Daddy had assurance he had helped someone in need. One day at church, a lady who had become a Christian came to Daddy, holding something tightly in her hand. She placed this in Daddy's hand. It was exactly the amount of the debt she had owed him for several years.

Daddy would take the shirt off his back if someone needed it more than he did. One day Mother saw Daddy in the linen closet gathering up some sheets. He was taking these sheets to someone that did not have any on their beds.

A compassionate person—this was my daddy!

16

Daddy's "Sticktoitiveness"

"Sticktoitiveness" is a word that best describes the legacy of my daddy. There is no way to remember how many times I have heard him say, "If you promise someone something—stick to it, even if it takes the skin off."

That was a rule he lived by to the nth degree. He also believed in staying with a job until it was finished. At times his perseverance made us worry about his health. Mother would sometimes say he took this too far—for his own good. Regardless of his occupation, plowing corn or planting cotton, slicing cheese or selling chickens, catching a bootlegger, or caring for a lost child; though weary and bone-tired, drenched in perspiration, he strived to do the best he could. His tenacious personality was the same in each. He was persistent in all endeavors.

He always put his hand to the plow and never looked back. Paul told us to live this kind of life, "Brethren, I do not count myself to have apprehended; but one thing I do, forgetting those things which are behind and reaching forward to those things which are ahead, I press toward the goal for the prize of the upward call of God in Christ Jesus" (Philippians 3:13-14).

Even when he was retired in his 70s and 80s, he would never stop until the last row in his garden was plowed, the last pea was shelled, or the last board was nailed in place, if at all possible. "Work as if you might live forever and live as if the Lord may come at any time" was Daddy's philosophy.

He always told my sister and me, "Always do the best you can, God doesn't expect more than that." When my sister was a child, she would start crying over some problem in her life. Dad would always say, "Now just wait a minute, things may not be as bad as they seem."

She would say, "I can't," and he would remind her that if she couldn't do it, God wouldn't expect her to do it.

He often reminded us to take one day at a time and not reach out for things to worry about that may never come. This was always a comfort to us as he lived this type of life before us.

When the tornado destroyed our home, store, and five buildings on our farm, people began to ask him what he was going to do.

He said, "I want to go back to O'Tuckolofa and build my house and store. When you have nothing left and you're down, there's no way to go but up."

This he did. Even though he had a very severe cut on his leg from the tornado and was on crutches, he rebuilt his store and home with the help of his friends.

Fast forward a few years.

After Daddy's years as sheriff were over, he and Mother decided to build a house in Oxford on our four acres, so we could all be together. He was looking forward to his retirement, when he could sit under a shade tree and play with his grandchildren. He could now enjoy the freedom from twenty-four hour telephone calls. There would be no more sleepless nights; there would be no more criminals to look for, and there would be no more people to take to mental institutions.

It didn't work out like that—the telephone did ring in about five months. Dad was being sued for $100,000! An ex-convict was suing on charges made during an arrest by officers not under Dad's authority. In fact, Daddy was in a Memphis hospital having surgery at the time this incident took place. Nevertheless, Dad was faced with this federal trial and the possibility of losing, for a second time, everything he owned.

Daddy told us again we would just have to depend on the Lord for strength, tell the truth, and let Him do the rest. After several long weary, tiring weeks, the trial was over. Dad won the case.

When spring came, he decided he would plant some corn. The cold weather got the first planting, and the second planting was eaten by the birds. It was the third planting that grew to be a lovely patch of corn. He was so proud of it.

He said one morning as he came by my house, "Come see my corn—it's seven feet tall and green as can be. It's going to make a world of corn."

Dad in corn patch.

A few days later a strong wind touched down and completely leveled over half of it. It was flat on the ground. As I stood gazing at the tasseled corn on the ground, I thought to myself—*I don't have the heart to tell him.* As I looked a little further into the field, I saw a stalk of corn move—there was Dad behind it, with his shovel, trying to put it up.

Another year he had a patch of corn ready to harvest, and the raccoons leveled a lot of it. They destroyed more than they ate. Again Daddy was in the patch early that morning, trying to salvage

as much as he could.

During these years we really had plenty of corn to supply our needs and then some.

In fact, we had so much that I was inspired to write about it.

COUNTRY CORN ON TOWN GROUND

I planted corn on an early morn,
One for the jay and a rainy day,
One for the crow and one to grow.

I plucked it and I shucked it,
Cut it by hand, put it in the pan,
What a feast to say the least.

I froze some corn on an early morn,
Corn in my chair, corn in my hair,
Corn everywhere, corn everywhere!

I breathed a sigh—come late July,
None to freeze, none to squeeze,
None to sell, none to shell.

I was not forlorn that early morn,
The squirrels had strewn what I had grown.
They ate the stuff, but I've had enough …
Of corn on an early morn.

There were so many good times on these four acres while Mother and Daddy were living. The children made many trips up the hill to visit them. Mother would help them with sewing, crafts, and taught them how to cook and freeze foods from the garden. They knew when they wanted a fried pie or a piece of cake they could find it at Granny's house. They also helped Daddy in the garden. We all had a part in growing all kinds of food such as watermelons, cantaloupes, popcorn, and all kinds of vegetables. Anson planted some pumpkin seeds in milk cartons. He transplanted them in the garden and watched them grow all summer. One vine grew up a tree about twenty feet high and had a very large pumpkin on it. Winds from a hurricane blew it down undamaged. When harvest time came, he had a total of 35 pumpkins. He had some to sell, give to neighbors, and plenty for his Granny to make pumpkin pies. He was so proud of the jack-o-lantern pumpkin he made that year.

Retirement did not end all problems—there were still more valleys and mountains. As I look back over my dad's life, I still marvel at how well he took those valleys, and how he showed us how to climb our own mountains by his faith and "sticktoitiveness." I hope I can pass this legacy on to my grandchildren and family.

He fought many health problems his last few years. Dad's faith and endurance was an encouragement to many people. We were blessed to be with him at home during his last years.

And Jesus said unto him, "No man, having put his hand to the plow and looking back, is fit for the Kingdom of God."

—Luke 9:62

(Top Left) Forest by his grandchildren.
(Top Right) Forest with friends on the square at the Courthouse in Oxford, Mississippi.
(Bottom Left) Dad with potatoes.
(Bottom Right) Anson with the pumpkins he and his Granddaddy raised.

17

The Little Red Button Box

The morning was clear, and the sun was almost ready to peep over the cedar trees in the backyard. It was, however, a bit chilly for a summer morning in the South. The car was packed, and Russ was ready to leave to attend a summer institute.

I was up early, getting together all the things I thought he might need, which he was sure to overlook. His lunch, maps, and other items had been placed on the front seat.

About this time our eleven-year-old daughter came out, rubbing her eyes. Her naturally curly hair was in little ringlets around her round face. She was determined to wake up early enough to tell her daddy good-bye.

"It's going to be a long summer without you around, Dad," she said, as she put her head in the car door to kiss him.

"You be a good girl and help Mother with all the chores, the dog, fish, chickens, and garden," he told her as he closed the door.

Standing there in the carport, we knew that before parting we must pray, as was the custom in our family before we took a trip. We prayed for the Lord's blessings upon each of us this summer. Our prayers started as oral prayers, but ended in silent ones. My voice had been silenced and there were tears in our eyes. As I put my arms around Debra, there were no more words, only the wave of our hands as he drove down the driveway and out of sight.

As I walked through the stillness of the house, I went into Anson's room. Our six-year-old son was sleeping soundly in bed, undisturbed by the shuffle of the early morning activities. I bent over and kissed his head, and whispered, "Sleep well, my son, you are the man of the house now, and we have a busy summer ahead."

"Oh, Mother, what are we going to do? Bible school is over, tennis and swimming will be no fun without Daddy, and I'm already tired of library books," Debra mumbled, as she went to her room and crawled into bed to get a few more winks of sleep.

I knew there was much resting upon my shoulders—the bills, mail, house, garden, and a four-acre city lot to keep in shape during the hot months ahead. I would have a large lawn to mow. I also knew there would have to be many and varied activities around our house to keep my eleven and six-year-old in peaceful harmony. Some everyday activities would automatically be struck from the routine by the absence of their daddy. Other projects were underway, but there would have to be more planned. Anson's four rows of popcorn were head-high and needed to be watered, which he liked to do late in the afternoon. There were vegetables of all kinds in the garden that needed to be gathered and put in the freezer. Debra had her jobs of caring for the aquarium and tropical fish, feeding and training the puppy she had recently gotten for her birthday, and also taking the scraps from the table each day to feed the chickens.

She still liked her chickens, because they were the Easter chicks from the past two years. She had two hens and a rooster of the older ones. Both hens were laying eggs.

She saved some of the eggs and put them into a homemade incubator. We made a wooden box with a piece of glass on top and put a light bulb in it above the eggs. A pan of water was also put inside the box and the temperature was kept between 100-103 degrees for a long twenty-one days. They had been attentive to turn the eggs one-half turn each day.

There was exuberance in the kitchen corner the day my children heard the first cheep of life in one of the eggs still unbroken. This was a very meaningful and unforgettable experience. Seven of the eight eggs hatched. Both children enjoyed feeding the tiny, yellow, fluffy chicks and watching them grow.

As the days passed, the freezer was about filled with vegetables, and the garden was still producing more than we could consume, even with the help of our friends.

One day I asked the children if they would like to set up a market on the street below the house and sell vegetables to people who passed by.

"Oh, boy, what do we need?" they asked. "Can we start right now?" they continued to inquire.

Those and a dozen more questions came so fast that I could not answer them, as excitement mounted. They were not long in letting their granddaddy know about their plans. He lived next door, so he began to help them with their new adventure. He helped them get a table placed in the shade of the big oak tree at the foot of the hill near the street. Debra rushed into the house for her paint set to make some signs. Anson hunted desperately for the baby scales to weigh the tomatoes, squash, and other vegetables. After he found the scales, he came into the kitchen with a box in his hand, and said, "Look, Mom, a money box. Will you give me some change to put in it?"

I could not help but notice that the little red box was the one he had just made in Bible School, painted all red, with a face on top made with buttons. He had been so proud to present it to me on the last night of Bible School.

I counted out $2.00 in change for him to put into the little red box. I reminded him, in a store business when you make some money, you pay back what you have borrowed.

"Sure, Mom," he said in a loud voice as he ran down the hill.

It was almost dark when

Debra and Anson's roadside vegetable market, along with visiting cousin, Cindy Harvey.

they finally brought their goods back to the house.

"Whew, am I tired," Anson remarked, as he fell across the couch.

"Me, too!" came from Debra, as she dropped to the floor in front of the TV, and began to watch one of her favorite cartoons.

Before they went to sleep they wanted to talk about their "store," and asked more questions. They had been so thrilled over their first-day sales. I told them their business would increase each day as more people learned of the market. I also reminded them of their responsibility to their customers, always to give good weight, never give mashed tomatoes, or bad ears of corn. They assured me that they would do their best.

"Wouldn't Dad be proud of us tonight if he knew about how we are selling vegetables from our own garden?" Anson said, as I tucked him into bed.

"Yes, dear, you'll have much to tell him when he gets home. Now get to sleep, for you will have another busy day tomorrow," I told him, as Debra joined us for our night time prayers together.

Business increased steadily and so did the August temperature. I saw them coming slowly up the hill one day and I thought to myself—this may be the vegetable market closing day.

"Mom, business is a bit slow, so we decided to put up a sign, BLOW FOR SERVICE, and then we'll run down when we have a customer," exclaimed Debra, as she wiped the perspiration from her face and reached for the glass of ice water I had waiting for them.

"Yes, that will be fine, and we can have that oil painting session I promised you," I told them.

We set up for the art session in the carport so they could see if a customer came. I gave them my oil paints, and they soon had their canvas and palette in hand. They were so absorbed in their painting that they didn't see a customer drive up. When she blew, they rushed down the hill. About halfway down, Anson stopped quickly and returned to the carport for the red box. They soon returned to the house.

"Oh, look, we sold a dollar's worth of tomatoes," Anson said, puffing out of breath, but waving the dollar bill.

"How many pounds did you give her?" I asked.

"Four," she answered.

"Two pounds for a quarter ...," and before I could finish, I could tell they realized a mistake had been made.

"Mother, what can I do? I don't even know her name," Debra said in distress.

"Don't worry, I think I recognized her and you can call her later," I told her.

"Can't I try now?" Debra pleaded.

"No, she won't be home for a while. We will call her later," I said.

The painting session continued, but I could sense the discontentment on Debra's face. Before night she had contacted the lady and told her to come by for her money or some more tomatoes.

There were many experiences they had in their little market that they always remembered. Much arithmetic and educational knowledge was obtained through this activity that they probably would not have received from their school textbooks.

Before the summer was over, Anson got a thrill out of mailing his daddy a few grains of popcorn that had actually partially popped open on the stalk from the 104-degree August sun.

They could hardly wait for the next day to arrive—for it was the day that their daddy would come home. They had so much to tell him. They counted and recounted the money they had made and packed it back in the red button box.

We had to go to town that day for a few minutes, but even so, the children were rushing me to get back home. They wanted to be home when their daddy arrived. On entering the driveway, they saw his car and saw him standing in the carport. We all jumped out of the car to greet him. Where was Anson? He had not greeted his daddy yet. Out the kitchen door he came, with outstretched arms, but tightly clutching the little red button box. He was so anxious to show his daddy all the money he had packed into it.

Later that day, they divided their money equally and handed me the $2.00 I had given them for change. I was glad they remembered to pay their debt, as in any business, but I thanked them and put it back in the box. Still later that day, I saw some money still in the box and I wondered why it was left.

The next Monday morning, as I was cleaning the house, I saw the red box and it was empty. At that moment I realized that the remaining money was probably taken to church on Sunday morning. When I asked about it, my thoughts were correct. They said, "Yes, Mother, that was our tithe money, we gave a tenth of what we made to the Lord." There was joy in my heart.

Everyone was back together once again. There was my mom and dad, my sister, my children, and Russ, back from his summer institute. I thanked the Lord for His blessings as I looked at the little red button box on the counter.

Russ and I walked across the newly-mowed lawn that I had so diligently tried to keep mowed during his absence. I looked at him and said, "Well, the summer passed faster than I had anticipated and we were greatly blessed, but it was no fun mowing all this grass—made me feel like a *grass widow*!"

> *Bring all the tithes into the storehouse,*
> *That there may be food in My house,*
> *And try Me now in this,"*
> *Says the LORD of hosts,*
> *"If I will not open for you the windows of heaven*
> *And pour out for you such blessing*
> *That there will not be room enough to receive it.*
> *—Malachi 3:10*

18

Mother's Day

Del and Myra's Mother, young and older.

My mother was one of the dearest and sweetest people in my life. Not only did she do so much for my sister and me during her lifetime, but for other people as well. She made clothes for relatives, and cooked and took food to people. Since she didn't drive, she used every opportunity to witness and serve the Lord at home or wherever she went. She spent much of her time sending cards and letters to friends who were sick, needed encouragement, or needed the Lord in their life.

I found a letter that I had written ten years after she died. It was on Mother's Day and she was very much on my mind. I put on paper some of my thoughts of her and what I would have liked to have said to her that day.

May 8, 1983
Mother's Day

Dear Mother,

Among my prized possessions, the other day I found some of your sweet letters written to me when I was away in college, when I married and moved to Oak Ridge, letters to your grandchildren, Debra and Anson, and other letters on special occasions.

They were all filled with such love, concern, and always filled with joyous anticipation for the day I would come home. Homecomings were always such happy times for us. I remember how you would always be at the door to welcome me. And when I get home for good—I don't know how close to the gate of glory you can stand, but I'm sure you'll be on hand to welcome me.

Your letters were such an inspiration to me, with words of counsel to help me stay on the straight and narrow way. I answered them all, but today I'd like to answer them again.

Yes, it's hard to believe you've been gone ten years. I know you need no letter, for you see quite clearly from Heaven's grandstand what is often so foggy to us who still run the race. A letter from me can give you little information, but one from you could certainly throw light on many a subject!

But just the same, I would like to thank you better than

I ever did when you were here, for the things you did and what you were to me. Even though you and Dad couldn't give me much of the world's goods those early years—you gave me things that money could not buy. I remember the Bible stories you read to Myra and me as we sat around the fireplace eating popcorn and peanuts. You would say prayers with us on bended knees on the cold floor. I would sometimes get tired and cold, but you would tuck us into bed and put a warm blanket around our feet. The first thing I would do upon returning from school each day was call, "Mother." You were always there to answer my call. You always made us pretty clothes to wear. You always had something good to eat when we got home from school. I remember those delicious cakes you made, and you would always let us have a hot piece of it as soon as it was baked, even though it was right before dinner.

I remember the crackers and vanilla flavoring bottle filled with water you would have tucked away in your purse to give me at church when I got restless—when I was too young to know the meaning of church.

Then I would put my head in your lap and go to sleep. I remember waking up on my way home one night as we rode home in a wagon. I saw a shooting star fall behind the trees, it seemed. I begged to get out of the wagon and go find it. You used this as an opportunity to tell me about the stars, the moon, the beautiful world God created, the Star of Bethlehem, and the Bright and Morning Star—Jesus Christ.

As I grew older, I often heard you praying for Myra and me in that little country store. Through the years I always felt your prayers—wherever I went, I knew your prayers went with me. You built a wall around my soul that the devil was never able to tear down. Even after you were gone, I still felt the power of your prayers.

As Brother Coleman took your Bible and read one of your prayers written in it, I looked at one of the pallbearers, the one that you had prayed for so often in this life—tears rolled down his face.

Since the Bible says in Luke 15:7, that joy shall be in Heaven over one sinner that repents, I feel you already know that he was saved a short time later. All this reminds me again of how important my prayer life should be.

I recall our last week together—we talked a long time about angels, and that the Lord sends angels to take His saints home to Heaven. Luke 16:22 says that the beggar died and was carried by the angels to Abraham's bosom.

That Saturday afternoon God sent His angels to carry you home. This, in a way, reminds me of the times I went to sleep in your arms at church, and you or Daddy would carry me home, only to awake sometime later and find I was home.

As I held you in my arms that afternoon when you breathed your last breath, and you lifted both your arms toward Heaven—all suffering, difficulties, and problems of this life were gone as you were carried into the splendor and grandeur of Heaven that await the true believer.

From that day, Mother, my life has not been the same. I had never felt the Holy Spirit like this before—could it have been I felt the brush of angels around me? From the looks of things down here, it may not be long until Jesus comes for all His saints. Oh, what a homecoming that will be!

In loving memory—
and all because of Jesus,

Your daughter, Del

Mother sewing.

Who can find a virtuous wife?
For her worth is far above rubies.

Her children rise up and call her blessed;
Her husband also, and he praises her:
                    —Proverbs 31:10, 28

Daddy and Mother.

19

A Letter Written by a Busy Mom

This letter was written to my sister, Myra, when she was teaching at Northwest Community College, around the mid-1970s. I had a son, Anson, in high school and a daughter, Debra, in school at Ole Miss. Russ, my husband, was a professor of Chemical Engineering at Ole Miss at this time. At the end of the letter you will be reminded of the CB radio jargon that was popular during the '70s. Many days were like this letter. Some of you can relate to the busy days of motherhood described here.

Tuesday, 9 a.m.

Dear Myra,

I'm sending this note to thank you for what you did for my birthday when you came home. Thank you so much for the good birthday dinner and cake, the shoes which I really adore, the lovely dress you made me, and all the numerous other things you do for me and my family. Daddy called Aunt Nora; she was feeling better. I need to go to the post office and mail her a card from him. Dorothy called today—they are all off to school.

A note about yesterday—

Before I got my night clothes off and dressed—I had breakfast, lunches made, and the family out the door. I heard some loud talking. Russ noticed that his car had leaked about a half tank of gas and was spraying out. He took my car and the children to school and went on to his classes. I had to have his car towed in, as they were afraid it might catch on fire if it was driven. I went to the garden and gathered greens, cooked dinner, listened to tapes, read and studied some—went to Dad's house to check on him. I borrowed a plunger from him to pump out the sewage lines, because the night before the water backed up in the tub, shower, and the commodes wouldn't flush. This was kind of bad managing this morning, but I got the water going out slowly. A lady called and wanted one of Debra's watercolor prints that I had promised her. I got to work shrink-wrapping it. Russ came home for lunch.

I drove him to the bank and then to school. I saw Debra and she wanted to come home and get some art tools she forgot this morning. I took her home and back to Ole Miss. On my way back, I went to the Law Building and made copies for my Bible Study. I picked up Anson, fixed his supper, and called a plumber. I took Anson and went to get Russ and Debra. I let them out at the repair shop to get his car. I took Anson on to his piano lesson and got home at 6:15 p.m. The plumber was here. I got shovels, lights, etc. to help him. A friend came by for Russ and they went to their carpenter class. It was time to take Debra to Navigator's Bible Study. The plumber left and said he would come back tomorrow. I took the art print to the lady at 8 p.m. I was late getting it to her, but she hadn't needed it and said that was OK.

I washed the dishes and went to get Debra at 9:30 p.m. Russ was home by now and had a splinter in his finger. I got it out!

Oh, during my leisure time I got to blow my nose, because

I had taken the worst head cold. Besides this, everything went off just fine and we had a great day. I was able to eat and my stomach only hurt part of the day.

I've only had one telephone call wanting something since I started this letter, so I will rush to get this to the post office, along with the other 16 letters and cards I wrote yesterday. I think it's just wonderful to be up and able to lead this busy life—when I think of those dear people I saw in the hospital Sunday. It is so sad to see some cry and not wish to live. Others are in a very sick condition. I thank the Lord everyday for His wonderful love, care, and blessings.

Thought you might get a chuckle out of yesterday's activities around the ole home 20. If Jennie Lee wants to give me a 10-20 about 8 p.m., on channel 4, I'll give her a 10-4. I'll be the "Ole Miss Butterfly" for the lack of a better name …

Have a good week!

Love You,

Del

20

The Lost Purse

"Mother, I've lost my purse!" Debra, my daughter, whispered to me as we stood in the crowded store.

"Where have you been in the store?" I asked her quickly.

"I have been all over the store, and I just don't know where I put it," she continued.

I rushed to the check-out counter and reported the lost purse to the manager. He was very kind and sent two clerks to help her look for it.

Within minutes, which seemed like hours, Debra came to me, smiling, with the purse over her shoulder. She had found it in a stack of blouses.

When I told the manager, he said, "You are lucky, most of the time we don't find them if they have been lost very long." We thanked him and breathed a sigh of relief as we went on our way.

A week later, Debra could not find her purse. After searching the house, she said she may have left it in the car.

No purse there.

"Maybe I left it in the restroom on campus," she then told me. We rushed to the campus and searched there—but her purse was not there.

"Maybe I left it in Daddy's office," she finally said.

I was getting more upset and worried as we waited to look in the office, which was closed at the time.

"How much money did you have in it? Oh, I hate for you to lose all your cards—social security, IDs, and driver's license. The purse alone would be about a twenty-five dollar loss," I commented in a perturbed voice.

Almost every coed who passed us had a brown leather purse over her shoulder. *Is that it?* we thought as each passed by.

Anxious moments passed as we waited for her daddy to come unlock his office. When he came, we rushed in and we were relieved to see that brown leather purse on his desk.

She put the purse in the car and rushed off to her physical education class. Since she lived at home and commuted to college each day, I decided to sit in the car and wait for her class to be over.

As I sat there, trying to relax from the searching, I stared at the small brown leather purse beside me. I thought of the day she bought it with her own money she had made from a painting she had sold. She was so proud of it.

I did not care to snoop into my daughter's personal belongings, but as I sat there I wondered what a thief would have found in my daughter's purse. Would there be something that one would not want others to see, read, or know about?

I emptied the contents of the purse on the car seat. This was what I found: a worn billfold containing eleven dollars, hair brush, sugarless gum, many well-used pencils, car and house keys on a hand-painted key ring, perfume, card calendar, football schedule and half of a football ticket, a card for three balanced meals and snacks, date book filled with class schedules and tests, a small Gideon New Testament, a book—*The Jesus Person Pocket Promise Book* by David Wilkerson, and a blue piece of paper with handwriting all over it.

I picked up the Gideon New Testament. Her name and the date she received it were inside the cover. Scribbled below, in her child-style handwriting, were these words, "I accepted Jesus Christ as my Savior in the fourth grade on my birthday, April 18, 1964.

A card pasted in the back of the Bible stated a simple Plan of Salvation. Opposite this was a small sticker that read, "Do not be worried or upset ... believe in God, John 14:1." Below this she had written, "We are on the winning side."

Tears streamed down my cheeks as I raised my head and looked across the Ole Miss campus as students rushed to and from class. I recalled that the morning paper reported several students who were arrested in drug raids. Some of those arrested were charged with multiple counts of narcotic law violations.

I looked back to the last item in the pile. I unfolded the blue sheet of paper that turned out to be the schedule for the Christian Student Fall Retreat that she had attended. The back of the sheet was completely filled with her handwritten notes, no doubt taken at the retreat. Two notes stood out above others as I read them. They were, "Don't live by feelings, but by the Word of God," and "A

Christian—you accept all of Jesus, the Holy Spirit comes to live in you—*forever*!"

A wonderful feeling came over me as I thought of these things a thief or even an honest person would have found. What a wonderful witness this purse would have been! Pride and joy flooded my soul as I wiped away more tears and returned the contents to the purse.

About that time Debra came bouncing out of the gym, smiling as always. Her face sparkled as she got in the car. "Guess what? I made twenty-eight laps around the gym today without stopping," she said, still puffing from the running.

I smiled with approval, but my thoughts lingered over the purse contents, as they reiterated that which I already knew—it was her love for God that put the fluorescent smile on her face, the twinkle in her eyes, and the bounce in her walk.

The lost purse helped me find my daughter anew!

What Is In Our Purse?

If we were to lose our purse today, what would we lose? Some things I'm sure would be hard to replace, such as our keys, Social Security Card, credit cards, Driver's License, money, checkbook, and medical cards. Maybe there would be the loss of pens, pictures, cosmetics, medicine, and jewelry.

Sometimes we don't appreciate things such as these until they are lost or gone, and we have to go to the trouble to replace them, if that is possible.

Our life, in some ways, could be compared to a purse and its contents. Is it filled with essentials or unnecessary things?

Do we carry the keys to doors of opportunity to reach people for Jesus? Do we use them often?

Do we carry a Spiritual Security Card with us today and for life eternal, knowing that we are secure in the Lord?

Do we carry a Driver's License that never has to be renewed, and allows us to travel on the straight and narrow roads that lead us on our journey here and to our final destination—Heaven?

Do we have a pen or pencil that will write down the service we need to render to our neighbors and to the lost? Does it have a good eraser to erase from our mind and heart the sins the Lord has forgiven us, when we repent and ask for His forgiveness?

Do we lay up too many earthly treasures? How many checks have we written and deposited in the Bank of Heaven?

Someday we will be asked to pour out the contents before God. What will He find?

Do not lay up for yourselves treasures on earth, where moth and rust destroy and where thieves break in and steal; but lay up for yourselves treasures in heaven, where neither moth nor rust destroys and where thieves do not break in and steal. For where your treasure is, there your heart will be also.

—Matthew 6:19-21

21

Brown Bag Lunch

There it was on the kitchen counter—a brown paper bag containing my teenager's lunch. I had made a special effort to prepare something different, because the day before he said, "Please, Mom, don't start making those banana sandwiches again this year!"

I had been up since 6:45 a.m., exercised my arms and legs, and was grateful to find they still moved. I went to the kitchen to prepare two lunches and breakfast for four people.

This morning was one of those mornings when you think, "Oh, me, what will I do first—if the phone doesn't ring, or if anything doesn't go wrong, maybe I'll make it." It was now 7:45 a.m. and silence filled the house. The garbage had not been taken out the day before, because my son had a late tennis practice, and did not have time to fulfill his chores. I decided to get that out of the way. I picked up the morning paper on the way back to the house. Before I had time to read the front page headlines the neighbor's dogs had distributed the garbage in various directions. I knew I must return to pick it up and put a concrete block on top of the garbage can. I rushed through the house, picked up the dirty clothes, and turned on the washing machine before I made my way back to the garbage pile.

I always dread for school to start, because the summer months have been so much fun; and it is always wonderful having the children around, going places, and doing things together. The first two or three months of school make some mothers of teenagers wonder how they are going to make it. There are always so many things to do, so many things to attend, and places to go. Oftentimes she needs to be at two places at the same time—and sometimes when she goes out to one of the two places, she finds she has no car. This particular morning fit into this category, except the car was still in the carport.

It was a lovely, sunny autumn morning, and I took my time listening to the birds, and watching a squirrel hiding acorns under the leaves for the winter ahead. A woolly bear caterpillar crossed the driveway in front of me, and I wondered if this meant another cold winter ahead. Some folks predicted the weather by the woolly bear. I could have spent the entire day in the yard, absorbing the fall beauty God had made, but duty called me back to the house.

Just as I got to the door, I stopped, looked down, and there was water trickling over the four-inch drop from the kitchen to the carport. Yes, the washing machine had overflowed and half the kitchen was already covered in water. A monumental clean-up job was ahead for me. After moving books, boxes, and art supplies, I finally got to the faucets, gathered towels, mops, and frantically went to work to save perishable items on the floor.

An hour later, I sat down exhausted, put my head back on the chair, and tried to relax. I looked into the kitchen, and on the counter I just couldn't believe what I saw. No, it couldn't be, because I positively remember saying as they were leaving, "Did you get your milk money and your lunch?"

There it sat—a brown paper bag with a delicious lunch inside. Should I just let him do without a lunch, or should I get up, dress, and make my way to the school? That just about did it for the morning. The teenage mother syndrome does catch up with us once in a while.

One mother I knew had to head for the clinic for tranquilizers at the beginning of each school year. The hustle and bustle was just too much for her. Another mother said she was not going to worry herself sick by trying to be at so many places at the exact time. I wondered how she could manage this, and then she told me her solution to the problem—she didn't wear her watch anymore.

Teenager's minds race in many directions. They often don't take on responsibilities as some parents think they should. Some parents tell how their teenagers always forget to put their car in park. One parent said this happened twice, causing the car to roll down their driveway and into the neighbor's yard, taking with it a share of trees and shrubs. Did your teenager ever forget to tell you they needed three dozen homemade cookies until two hours before they were to be served? Have they ever locked the car keys in the car? Just wait until they lock them in the trunk of the car and do not have extra keys. Maybe they have left their chemistry notebook at school the night before they are to take a nine weeks test the next day. Have they ever left the stove oven on all night? Did you ever jump to your feet to think the house was on fire, only to find the curling iron still plugged in and touching some combustible material?

One day the phone rang and a panicky voice said, "Oh, Mother, I forgot the thousand soda straws I was supposed to bring to class. Would you please run over to the supermarket and rush them out to me at the Art Building as soon as possible?"

"But what …?"

"Thanks, Mom."

A thousand soda straws—that must be some big party, I thought. I turned off my dinner and rushed to the store. There weren't many boxes left when I filled my basket. I found out later they were for an art project.

I finally made myself get up. I put his name on the brown lunch sack and drove to school. The first time is not bad, the second time is no fun, but the third time, you really hate to ask the school secretary to have the lunch sent to your son again.

But when I handed it to her, she just smiled pleasantly, and said she would be happy to get it to him before lunch time.

I breathed a sigh of relief over my morning's work, realizing I had not done one thing I had planned to do. I guess the other things were not important, because I couldn't remember a single one of them.

As I drove home, the sky was still blue, and I, too, smiled as I looked up and said out loud, "This is the day which the Lord has made; I will rejoice and be glad in it." As I thought of my two wonderful, precious children who had committed themselves to Christ at a young age, and had continued to be faithful in His service—how thankful I was!

The brown lunch sack syndrome will pass with the passing years. Teenagers will sometimes fail, fret, and forget, but parents must return the failures and forgetfulness with patience, pardon, and praise. They will clutter the house and sometimes do the impossible, but this is all a part of growing up. In a home where there is much love for each other, and where Jesus Christ is Lord, they will grow into lovely adults—maybe sooner than we realize.

Before I realized it, school was out that day and my six-foot teenage son came in the door. He bent down and placed a kiss on my forehead and said, "Thanks, Mom, that was a great lunch you sent me by special delivery!"

That was all I needed to wrap up this busy day! I thanked the Lord for the blessings of children, especially my two precious teenage children!

Behold, children are a heritage from the LORD,
The fruit of the womb is a reward.
Like arrows in the hand of a warrior,
So are the children of one's youth.
Happy is the man who has his quiver full of them;
They shall not be ashamed,
But shall speak with their enemies in the gate.
—Psalm 127:3-5

22

Empty Boxes— Empty Hearts

My daughter, who was a teacher, came home one day from school with the following story that she could not forget.

It was nearly Christmas time and the teacher in a special education third grade class had her students help decorate a tree. The next day the teacher had placed several bright, beautifully-wrapped packages under the tree. The students were all smiles when they saw the packages. One little girl just couldn't keep her hands off the ribbons and bows. She often stood gazing and wondering what was in each package. She lingered in the room after all the other students and teacher went out for recess. She rushed up to the tree and grabbed the most beautifully-wrapped package. She ran back to her desk, put it in her lap, and hurriedly opened the box.

The students soon returned to the room. After everyone had settled down, the teacher heard someone sobbing in the back of the room. As the teacher approached the little girl, she started crying profusely, as if her heart would break. Before the teacher asked about her problem, she saw the crumpled Christmas wrapping, untied bow, and the empty box.

The packages were not presents at all—only empty boxes that the teacher had placed under the tree for decorations. The little girl's great anticipation and expectation had now ended in such disappointment that she could not contain her heartbreak. She knew she had done something wrong, and then to find an empty box was more than she could take.

Christmas finds some people like this little girl, holding empty boxes, some with empty stomachs, empty purses, and empty hearts.

The greatest Christmas joy is not found in packages, but in people, not in shops, but in sharing, not in gifts, but in giving—giving of ourselves!

God gave us the greatest gift of all 2,000 years ago, when He gave us His Son, Jesus—Savior, Emmanuel—God with us.

What a blessing it is to know that our life can be filled with His spirit and His love.

God with us, this is the real meaning of Christmas. If He is living with us and in us, our hearts can never be empty.

23

The Empty Nest

I have seen eastern bluebirds in my yard in January and February, looking over the nesting boxes. I'm not sure where they go after they spend a few days going in and out of the box in the middle of winter.

When a few warm days come, and the grass begins to show through the brown stubble, the bluebirds return and get busy

building their nest with twigs and pine needles. They then line it with feathers or soft material. Then come the days when the Mother bluebird is not seen very much, and the Papa bluebird sits on top of the box or in a tree nearby. He seems to be guarding the nest when the Mama bluebird is inside.

The busy, busy days come as both are seen going in and out of the nest every few minutes for many days. They are taking healthy meals of bugs and worms to their little ones.

Before long, I see little heads peeping out into the sunlight of a big world. They cheep and chirp loudly when their food does not arrive on time. They get impatient and poke their heads out of the nest, hoping to be the first to receive a juicy morsel of food.

I try to take a few still camera shots of them each year, as well as a few videos. One day I missed a shot of a lifetime.

The time had come for the baby birds to leave the nest, and one after the other took the plunge into the air, and their little wings began to flap very fast. One landed on the ground, but some of the stronger ones made it to a tree nearby. This put an extra responsibility on Mama and Papa to have their young ones scattered, but still needing to be fed. All had tried their wings, except one little late bloomer. It was fearful, wanting to leave the nest, but not sure about what was in store on the outside.

Papa bluebird tested the little one on several occasions by withholding the food, but he finally gave in. The next day Papa flew to the nest with what appeared to be a huge grasshopper. He held his head back, as the baby reached outside the hole in the box to get it, but to no avail. On a second try it came out of the nest far enough to get a hold on the food. The instant it did, Papa pulled away from the box and out came the baby, still holding on and flapping its little wings very fast. Papa flew backwards, turning loose of the food in midair. The baby landed on the ground and enjoyed its dinner.

Days went by and one day I saw five small bluebirds on top of the bluebird house. They all came home after being away for a while.

As the bluebirds knew when it was time to leave the nest, so it is with our children. Oh, how we dislike seeing them leave home, yet we know there comes a time when they must go away to live their lives somewhere else, to college, work, or somewhere to have their own home and family.

Our two children left home within seven months of each other, and, to say the least, it was a lonely time. They had been home with us for twenty-two and twenty-seven years. As these little birds did, we sometimes say children leave their nest and go out, trying out their wings. Some parents get the empty nest syndrome when they don't hear footsteps and everything is so quiet around the house. Then there is an empty place or two at the table. This is especially hard on a stay-at-home Mom, who has been so close to her children for those many years. We always had so much fun in the summer when they were at home. I have heard some mothers say, however, they will be so glad when their children go back to school. This thought never crossed my mind. It was such a blessing to have my children home.

Not only do we as parents feel depressed and sad over the empty nest, but many children are sad and get homesick when they leave home. They finish high school and go away to college or work. If they have not had the right training at home during their formative years, they sometimes get in trouble. I remember hearing of a beautiful girl who went out with the wrong boy, who was drinking and had a car accident that left her a cripple for life. It is so sad when young people make wrong choices and have to suffer a life of pain and heartache. The baby bluebird didn't have much choice that day, because it was hungry, and it knew it had to hold on for dear life as it was pulled from the nest. At the time, I imagined it thought Papa was being cruel to it.

When my sister went to college and away from home, she was very homesick. Daddy stopped by to see her one day and she began to cry, begging him to let her go home with him and quit college. He always had a way of reconciling us in troubled times. He told her things would get better, and she could come home for a visit in a few weeks. He finally left her in better spirits. If he had given in to her desire, she probably would never have gone to college again.

She often looked back on this time and was so thankful that Daddy insisted that she remain in college.

Our two children lived at home while in college. They never desired to live on campus or in an apartment. Russ was a professor at Ole Miss at this time, and their tuition was free; and by staying at home, this saved money. They liked having good meals at home, as well as their laundry and ironing being done by Mama.

The empty nest leaves a mother and father the extra time to let the Lord lead them into new horizons and service for Him. Also, the older we get, we welcome the fact that we don't have as much work to do. There is also the joy of homecomings from college, work, and then come the blessings of that wonderful day when they return with their own children to visit with a very happy grandmother and granddaddy.

Train up a child in the way he should go,
And when he is old he will not depart from it.
                                   —Proverbs 22:6

24

Home for Christmas

Twelve days until Christmas and there was so much to do. With plans to make, places to go, presents to buy, Christmas cards to send, visits to make, and baskets to deliver. Sometimes life is stressful, even though we have a smile on our face.

Sometimes we get tired. We get tired of writing cards, buying presents, decorating, cooking, working in the house, running errands, and doing "good things."

Today was one of those days. I was tired, really tired—and depressed. I wished for a retreat far away, where I could sit out the rest of the twelve days, or part of them, at least, to be alone and relax. It seemed there would be no better time than now.

Since I have my own four-acre backyard retreat, I don't have to go very far to be alone. Today was a warm December day and the sun was bright against the cloudless blue sky. I lay down on the grass. It was warm and I relaxed—just God and me on my little plot of land I call Aven's Haven. It was exceptionally quiet, except for the occasional pecking of a pileated woodpecker on a dead pine tree, and a squirrel or two scampering up and down a tall oak tree.

It was two o'clock in the afternoon, but through the webbed branches of a hickory tree, the moon could be seen as it moved toward the western sky. It was a time to reminisce, to praise the Lord for His precious gift of Jesus, and to ask for that special touch from Him that I needed at this time. I thought of His words, "Be still and know that I am God." I didn't feel guilty with any thoughts that

I could be wasting time, because it was time with Him in prayer and meditation.

My bones needed to move. I got my gloves, clippers, and pulpwood saw, and started on that path that had led my children so many years in search of that special cedar Christmas tree. I made my way through the bramble, bushes, and briers. I crossed the weeds that had grown over the pet cemetery where ducks, chickens, quail, Chee-chee, Sweetie Pie, Runt, and all the rest had been laid to rest. Do you have one of these?

Along the barbed wire fence boundary line, I chopped from my path blackberry vines, grape vines, honeysuckle, and small cherry trees. The path had once been well-trodden by my dad on his way to the corn patch. I finally came to the opening path where he raised the delicious sweet corn and blue lake beans.

I continued to stroll along Burney Branch, where white sand and pebbles lined the creekbed. Along the banks, entwined in the bushes, and up the trees were many muscadine vines. It was here that my children gathered seventeen gallons of muscadines one September. We had muscadine pies, muffins, and marmalade— muscadines to freeze, muscadines to squeeze, and lots to give away.

As I walked along the bank of the creek, I spotted the place where my special black walnut and dogwood trees were supposed to be, only to find that both had died and fallen to the ground. They had lived out their lives, but I noticed in this area were many young walnut and dogwood trees that were ready to burst forth with new life in the spring. I continued to walk around these four acres.

The garden fence was gone. There was no garden. The swingset frame was rusty and hidden behind some maple trees. The brown dormant grass covered the lawn that was once dirt from the pounding of many little feet playing football, softball, croquet, and badminton.

This same spot was covered with snow many years ago at Christmas and was a beautiful winter playground for my children. There were snowball fights, the snowman in all its splendor, boots on, boots off, snow suits on, snow suits off, along with puddles of melted snow all over the kitchen floor. There were cold little hands, but warm hearts, waiting for bowls of vanilla snow ice cream. This was the highlight of the day.

During my walk I recalled other events—the excitement of the Christmas parade, waiting in the cold with the children, making pictures with Santa at Sears, shopping for a special teacher, and making cookies for the school class parties.

It will soon be Christmas again, and the children will soon be coming home. We will feast at noon and then gather around the piano and sing our favorite Christmas carols.

We will then open our gifts, one at a time. Sometimes the oldest member of the family gets to open their gifts first, and sometimes the youngest. There is joy in Aven's Haven when the children come home for the family reunion!

It will soon be time to start cooking for this special day. Home for Christmas, what sweeter words, what greater joy could we hear?

If you still have a Mom or Dad to go home to be with, how blessed you are. If you have children or grandchildren, what a joy it is to say, "My children and grandchildren will be home for Christmas." If you have children living at home with you now, enjoy every minute you can with them. Enjoy every toy you have to fix, every place you have to take them, every book you read to them, every little league baseball game, even the piano lessons, and all the hundred other things you have to do for them and with them. It seems such a short time ago that Russ and I were buying Christmas toys.

I also remember when my sister and I would be coming home from college to be with our parents. Homecoming days were wonderful. Our parents have gone on to their glorious home in Heaven to celebrate Christmas forever with Christ the Lord.

I have seen many Christmases come and go, some sunny and some with fallen snow, but each one becomes more precious and sweeter the older I grow—and all because of Jesus, God's greatest gift to us. I don't want to miss Christmas, do you?

I didn't find a Christmas tree today, but I received a greater reward. After walking with the Lord and remembering "Christmas past" and spending time alone with Him, I was now ready to enter the reality of today with new strength for the glorious day of our dear Savior's birth.

As I headed back to the house, counting my blessings, in the distance I heard the church chimes playing "Joy to the World! The Lord is come." This day had brought much joy and many blessings to me!

25

Caregiver

"... 'Assuredly, I say to you, inasmuch as you did it to one of the least of these my brethren, you did it to Me'."
—*Matthew 25:40*

There have been at least eight very special people in my life that I have helped as a caregiver—some for a brief time and some for several years. I have been blessed with health and strength to be able to help care for these loved ones.

I had prepared for a profession of teaching. After I graduated from Ole Miss, with BAE and MAE degrees in Education, I taught for six years. I taught fifth and sixth grades and also algebra in high school. After I married and had a precious baby girl, I knew my teaching career was over.

This was my first caregiver job. I had to be home with my little girl. Five years later, our precious baby boy was born. During all the years of their young lives we never hired a babysitter. We were blessed to have my parents and sister living next door much of this time. When it was necessary for us to go somewhere without our children, they stepped in as wonderful babysitters, loving every minute of it.

During these years, I knew I had the best job I could ever have. I was always paid with love, hugs, and kisses from my precious children. I could have had a good salary teaching, but I chose to do without some material things to be with them. When they were both in school and were walking through the school doors, I said to myself, "There goes my everything!"

We had to take our children to school and pick them up each day. The bus only transported children who lived outside the city. They both lived at home until they graduated from Ole Miss.

When the children were still small, my mother had a heart attack and was in the hospital for twenty-one days. I helped my sister and Daddy care for her. She was not in good health for the next eight years. It was hard to have to give up a precious mother at sixty-eight years of age.

During Mother's last years, her mother—my grandmother, had a stroke and had to go to a nursing home. The family tried to care for her at home, but could not. Since my mother was not able to help, I tried to help the rest of the family in her place.

I went to visit with her several times a week to chat with her and check on her needs. Debra went with me when she wasn't in school. "Granny" as we called her, was a wonderful grandmother. She said to me one day, "Oh, how I wish I could get out of this wheelchair and help these old folks!" When she mentioned how she wanted to help others, I knew her heart, but I told her it was now her time to start receiving help and gifts.

She had been the type of person that helped other people, taking them

Del's Grandmother, Josie Harvey.

food or other things that they needed. She always had a glass of iced tea or a fried pie for the mail carrier or anyone who came to her house. She knitted house shoes for many people and sold some to give money to the church. I gave her a large-print Bible that I thought she needed. I went by her house one day, not long after this, and saw she was reading from her old Bible. She told me that her neighbor down the street needed the Bible more than she did, and she gave it to her. Many times I would go to her house and I would think she had visitors, only to learn she was actually praying and talking out loud to the Lord. When people said something about her living alone, she always said, "No, I'm not alone, God is always with me."

I went to visit my grandmother one day, and she was out in the front yard. She said she had just found her house key there in the yard. She said she had looked in the house and couldn't find it. She then remembered that she had not prayed about it. When she did, the Lord directed her to the front yard. She told me this as she held up her key.

At this same time, Russ had an aunt who lived alone and was not in good health. We lived closer to her than her daughter or sisters. We went to see her often to check on her and see about her needs. She had a cook and housekeeper part of the day. She really liked mustard and turnip greens. We always had plenty in our garden. My children and I kept her supplied with them. I often said we had taken her enough greens over the years that, if put together, would have filled her entire kitchen. We were happy to run errands and do things for her. At this time, grocery stores, drugstores, and the dairy would make deliveries to your house. Milk was delivered in quart glass bottles to your door as often as you needed it. They would pick up the empty bottles each time they delivered the milk.

Russ's aunt had her medicine and other drugstore needs delivered often. One day she called the drugstore and said, "Mr. Gathright, do you have any secrets?"

There was a long silence, and finally he said, "Mrs. Frazier, what did you say you wanted?"

From the back of the house, her daughter hollered and said, "Mama, it is not secrets, it's *Sucrets*!"

She then told him, "You know, those little mints in a small tin box."

"Oh, you want some *Sucrets*. Yes, ma'am, we have them and will send them to you right away," he said. She was often kidded about asking Mr. Gathright if he had any secrets.

After Mother died, Daddy lived alone for several years. As he grew older, he had to have several surgeries. Myra quit her teaching job, and we shared the care for him. He had to have gastrostomy surgery, and was fed liquids or liquids mixed with baby food through a tube in his stomach for over three years. He could not walk, but we used a hydraulic lift to roll him from his bed to the den, where he would read or watch TV. His mind was good, and he enjoyed talking to friends and family who came by to see him. It was so hard for him to smell food, and not be able to eat or drink anything by mouth, not even a swallow of water. The cancer he had at age fifty-six may have caused his problems, but he lived to be almost eighty-six years old. He took all his hardships so well, remaining strong in his faith and looking to the blessed hope of life eternal with the Lord.

Jesus said, "Whoever drinks of this water will thirst again, but whoever drinks of the water that I shall give him will never thirst. But the water that I shall give him will become in him a fountain of water springing up into everlasting life" (John 4:13-14).

Soon after I was a caregiver for my daddy, Russ's mother broke her hip. We cared for her at our house until she could walk and go back to her house. She soon broke her other hip and was back in our care again. At this time we pleaded with her to live with us, but she wanted to go home. She was ninety-eight years old. She lived about twenty miles away, but we went to see about her at least once a week or more. She had wonderful neighbors who checked on her often. They watched to see if her window shades went up every morning.

One day they called to tell us that her shades were not up, and we had better come see about her. We found her alive, but on the floor in the kitchen. She had suffered a stroke and could not move parts of her body and could not talk.

After her stay in the hospital, she had to come live with us. Our dining room was made into a bedroom with a hospital bed. I was able to check on her often when I was working in the kitchen. She could not walk or talk, but she could use her hands. Even though she could not talk, she always had a way of letting us know her needs. We would put her in a wheelchair for most of the day. She would sit and watch Laurel and Hardy or other old movies and laugh out loud.

The only thing she said, during her two years and four months with us following her stroke, was to our son, Anson. He had been skiing or hiking in the mountains and was here visiting. He talked to her about his trip. He said, "Grandmother, one day in the mountains I saw a mother bear and her little cub."

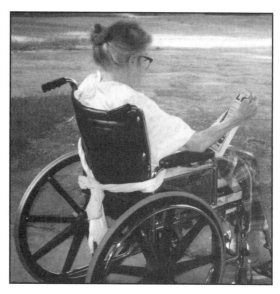

She looked up at him, smiling, and said, "A mother bear and a baby bear." That was a thrilling moment for all of us. That was the last and only thing she said.

Russ's Mother, Clara Aven.

Friends and family came to our house on July 10, 1997, and celebrated her 100th birthday, before the Lord called her home at 101 years old.

One year during her time with us, my sister, Myra, had to have aorta heart surgery in Birmingham, Alabama. I had to leave Russ caring for his mother, and go to be with Myra during this serious heart surgery. She had complications following surgery, and we were there for 28 days. Russ had some home health care help with his mother, but it was discontinued part of the time, while I was gone. He was full-time caregiver now, with little or no help.

When I finally got home, I was now caregiver at my house and Myra's house that was next door. The Lord blessed her and she recovered from this surgery.

Shortly after this time, something wonderful happened! It was Christmas Eve, and I held a precious eleven-month-old baby girl in my arms. I was a grandmother at seventy-two years of age. The gentle embrace of this little baby was an indescribably joyful experience. My daughter, Debra, was teaching school at the time the good news came. Debra and John traveled to China to get this little girl. Soon after baby Abbey arrived, Debra asked me if I could help care for my granddaughter a while, as she finished the final days of the spring semester. She wanted to teach until they found a teacher to replace her. She was teaching in the Gifted Education Program. What a joyful time we all had, taking care of Abbey in our home and in her home as well. Even though I was a caregiver for this precious little girl for only a short time, it brought back memories of my two children.

During this time, Myra was having problems walking because of her hip. The day came when she had to have hip replacement surgery. She made it through the surgery with no problems, but the next day when the nurses were trying to get her up, she had a stroke. I stayed with her in the hospital for 45 days. I did have some help when I needed a break or to come home for some rest. When she was able to walk some on a walker, she came to our house for the rest of her life, which was five years.

She had Long-Term Health Care insurance, which was a wonderful help. I had additional assistance for about five hours a day—five days a week. The rest of the day and night she was in my care. She was able to walk slowly, with her walker, as we held on to a wide belt she had to wear. She missed the use of her right hand to write, sew, do embroidery work, and knit. She learned to write some with her left hand. The stroke did not affect her mind, so she liked to read, watch TV, and always enjoyed friends and relatives who came to visit her. She had several wonderful caregivers. One was Kay, who was a former beautician. She would cut and set Myra's hair and manicure her nails just the way she liked. She was very special to Myra. Another caregiver was Dee, who liked to cook. She cooked delicious meals which Myra liked. She was also very special to Myra. Another caregiver, Hazel, was with her for several years, and they had a good time together. They laughed and talked and laughed some more! We often repeated Proverbs 17:22, "A merry heart does good, like medicine."

Myra and Hazel.

Most mornings we greeted each other with this verse:

This is the day the LORD has made;
We will rejoice and be glad in it."
                    —Psalm 118:24

Hazel helped Myra and all of us so much during these years. Everybody around here loved Hazel.

Myra was able to go to church, using her walker.   She

sometimes went shopping with me, in her wheelchair; but most of the time, in cooler weather, she sat in the car.

She had to have several other surgeries during the years following her stroke, including cataract, carpal tunnel, and radio frequency ablation.

Our son, Anson, was diagnosed in 1999 with myelofibrosis, an incurable disease. He had a life expectancy of three to five years. I went with him to Mayo Clinic in Rochester, Minnesota three times. I also went with him to a number of clinics, doctors, and cancer centers, where he had many blood transfusions, and several surgeries. These were really hard times on our family. Russ was a great help through all of the years I was a caregiver. When I had to be away from home, he was always here to see to the needs of Myra or other family members.

It took over an hour to drive to Anson's house; and I made many trips to help him, then I traveled back home to do my other tasks. During the last months of my son's life, in 2007, I was with him much of the time. The last trip to Mayo Clinic was in February

Anson in hospital bed joking around—squirting Debra
with a syringe full of water.

2007. It was a cold trip there and back. At this point his spleen was so enlarged, due to his disease; that it had to be removed, even though he knew he could not live long without it. He took his suffering so well.

He and the doctor, known as the "spleen king," talked about how much Anson's spleen would weigh. The doctor came in after the surgery and said it weighed 29 pounds, the largest he had ever removed in all his years of practice. Anson had made a record at Mayo Clinic! About three months later, he developed AML (Acute Myeloid Leukemia) that ended his life at the age of forty-six. That was seven years and eight months after he was diagnosed with myelofibrosis. It was hard to give up our precious son, as some of you know, who have had to give up a child.

Within one year, between 2006 and 2007, Russ and I had to give up seven of our loved ones.

One morning Myra was sitting on the side of her bed. She slid off and hit her leg and head on her motor chair. She had a small knot on her leg, with a tiny red spot on her head, no bigger than a dime, and no knot at all. I took her to the Urgent Care Clinic to check on her leg and she became unconscious. She was sent to the hospital immediately and had surgery for bleeding on the brain. She had been taking Coumadin since her heart surgery. This, no doubt, caused the bleeding. She lived only a few days after the surgery. I had to give up my sister on May 15, 2010, at age eighty-three. I was blessed to have had a sister for eighty-one years of my life.

I will mention two more caregiving jobs that I had for a short period of time.

Russ had a couple of surgeries, but soon recovered. Debra was in an automobile accident and had broken bones. She also had major surgery a few years ago. She stayed with us for a few weeks after each of these illnesses.

I didn't always choose the caregiver profession, but it kept on choosing me. I shall be thankful that, as a family, we were always together. The Bible speaks of caring for family members, and what a joy and privilege it was to be with them until they entered their permanent heavenly home. Our peace and joy comes in knowing where they are and who they are with. They finished well at home with loved ones. In the cemetery, not far from our house, are four marker-monuments in a row—my mother, daddy, son, and sister. There is one unusual marker among the four. Anson liked to go hiking in the mountains. He liked the rocks he saw along the way; in fact, he enjoyed all of God's creation. He wrote in his eulogy that he wanted to have a large rock for his grave marker. He wrote down the kind and the size. It is definitely one of a kind in this cemetery.

I thought of the rocks mentioned in the Bible. "… You are my rock and my fortress; …" (Psalm 31:3). Another reference is "… When my heart is overwhelmed; Lead me to the rock that is higher than I" (Psalm 61:2).

I don't go to the cemetery very often, because I know my loved ones are not there; but one of these days we will all be caught up to meet Jesus, our Lord and Savior, in the clouds. We will be with our family once again, but best of all, we will be with our Lord forever.

For the Lord Himself will descend from heaven with a shout, with the voice of an archangel, and with the trumpet of God. And the dead in Christ will rise first. Then we who are alive and remain shall be caught up together with them in the clouds to meet the Lord in the air. And thus we shall always be with the Lord. Therefore comfort one another with these words.
—1 Thessalonians 4:16-18

I am the way, the truth, and the life. No one comes to the Father except through Me.   —John 14:6

Our mission and goal is to be an observant caregiver. What I mean by this is to care enough to tell the lost how to be saved, so that they too may have the blessed hope of a life with Jesus for all eternity.

26

Caregiver Stories

One day Myra went to the hospital for outpatient surgery. That is right, she was *out* all afternoon!

As I sat in the waiting room, I looked the room over, and saw only one picture frame on the wall. In the frame was an Ole Miss baseball shirt with a large number on it. As I looked at the shirt, I thought that must have been a young boy who was an *out* patient who lost his shirt!

****

One night when Myra was in the hospital, the nurse told her she couldn't have any medicine for sleep until 12:30 a.m.

Across the hall a lady screamed and hollered nonstop, at the top of her voice. We prayed for her, considered putting Kleenex in our ears, and towels under the door. At about 3:30 a.m., without any sleep at all, I pressed the button for the nurse. She answered, "May I help you?"

"Yes, ma'am, we would like to have two good sets of earplugs," I told her.

There was a long silence and in a very subdued voice she said, "I'm sorry, we don't have any." Then she went on to say that the yelling was the only way this lady had of communicating with them. I hadn't said a word to the nurse about the reason we weren't sleeping.

About fifteen minutes later, a nurse came in our room and said the lady had gone to sleep—we knew it had gotten quiet. I said, "Well, that's good, but we aren't asleep; could Myra have a Tylenol PM?"

She said, "I'm sorry, we can't give any sleep medicine after 4:00 a.m." and she left. As tired and sleepy as we were, we laughed about the events of the night. Myra turned over and soon went to sleep.

I put my head down on my jacket that I had rolled up for a pillow and prayed, *Lord, please keep me alive while I'm still living!*

****

Myra was in the hospital and had broken out in a rash. The doctor made his rounds, saying he would order some allergy medicine for it, and he would check on her the next morning. We waited and waited and no medicine came. I called the nurse and she said it hadn't "come up" yet. Again we waited a long time, but still no medicine came. I called the hospital pharmacy and found out that none had been ordered.

Finally, the nurse came to the room to check on Myra, but with no medicine. As she started to leave, I said, "If some Benadryl or allergy medicine is not sent up soon, I am going to be compelled to call Doctor Aven and personally have him bring some to us."

She turned around quickly, looked at me, and said," Who is Dr. Aven?"

I said, "He is my husband" (PhD, not an MD). When she left, we had a good laugh. The medicine "came up" real soon!

****

I talked with a lady who had been a caregiver for her husband for several years. He had Alzheimer's disease and she couldn't leave him alone. She recently had fallen and broken her arm.

She had a daughter living with her who was not in good health. This was one of those cases where the caregiver needs a caregiver. So many people have very difficult times caring for their loved ones at home.

My family talked about the fact that there may come a time when the family would not be able to care for each other. We all agreed, and were in one accord, that we would take care of each other as long as we were able. Then, when and if the time came when we couldn't, we would go to an assisted living facility or nursing home.

One day I visited a cousin of mine in an assisted living center. She was very happy there. She said she didn't have to fix three meals a day, clean house, get the yard mowed, and many other things that she was not able to do. She had many friends there to visit and talk with. She said she doesn't need a TV for entertainment. She sews, embroiders, writes, reads, and seems so happy in this environment. She is still able to go to church and participate in other activities. It is wonderful to know our loved ones are happy and well cared for.

****

I believe a caregiver at home, in a hospital, a clinic, or flying from place to place has a great opportunity to meet and talk with other people in need. When a person has a great need in their life, they will be ready or more willing to receive a tract, or listen to one's testimony about the Lord. As the title of Jane Eggleston's poem says, "It Is In The Valleys I Grow."

My family had many opportunities during these caregiving years to talk and witness to many people. There were always people who needed encouragement. They may have needed a Bible, a tract, or a listening ear. Debra and I have written a few tracts, and for many years Debra designed our Christmas cards. During all these years I have had only two people refuse our cards or other tracts. One lady refused the Christmas card, saying she didn't celebrate Christmas. The other person was on a plane going across country to her grandmother's funeral. She refused my tract and let me know she didn't want to hear anything about God or Jesus.

While I was a caregiver in several hospitals, I wrote Bible verses on the blackboard or bulletin board. At one hospital we had a doctor who was retired, but filling in for another doctor. He often glanced at the verse on the board and began a very helpful devotional. We always looked forward to the words of comfort and his prayers of encouragement for the day.

One day I put some of my thoughts on a piece of paper and put it on the outside of our door. Later that afternoon, a nurse came in and said, "That was meant for me today. Thank you so much!"

Sometimes we think the only ones that need help are the ones in the bed. Many doctors, nurses, aides, and caregivers need words of encouragement and inspirational motivation. I always tried to keep a supply of tracts in the hospital on the shelf by the window. Often the lady who cleaned the room would pick up one and thank us as we thanked her for helping care for our needs.

Therefore ... be steadfast, immovable, always abounding in the words of the Lord, knowing that your labor is not in vain in the Lord.   *—1 Corinthians 15:58*

Confess your trespasses to one another, and pray for one another, that you may be healed. The effective, fervent prayer of a righteous man avails much.   *—James 5:16*

27

International Student Ministry

Group of international students.

In the mid-1980s, Dorothy, my aunt, Myra, my sister, and I taught about twelve international students over a period of time. We would meet at the church one afternoon each week for a conversational English class. We also studied the Bible as part of the class. The students were from Malaysia, China, Japan, Korea, Vietnam, and Yugoslavia. We gave them bilingual Bibles and other easy-to-read English Bibles. Several of the students came to church and Sunday school.

Mark and Paul, Vietnamese "boat people," accepted Christ and were baptized at our church before they left.

Misa, from Yugoslavia, gave her Bible back to us, saying she could not take it back to her country. In fact, her husband didn't want her to have it. Near the end of her time at Ole Miss, she kept one of the Bibles. I believe she concealed it from him and took it to her country. Today, I can only hope and pray she kept the Bible and has freedom to read and use it in her country.

Stephanie, from Taiwan, was faithful to come to church, and we knew she was growing in her understanding of the Word. She could not get her husband, John, to come with her to church. Stephanie and John had a baby boy born to them while in Oxford. I gave her the children's book I had written, *God Has Special Places*. When I visited her in the hospital, she said, "We will name our baby Timothy, the same name in your book and in the Bible."

A Christmas card came to me from Stephanie in Oklahoma City, December 1989, with a note that said, "I have two big things to share with you. First, my husband and I were baptized last September 24th. Thank the Lord! We go to Calvary Chinese Baptist Mission now. There are two Chinese Baptist Missions in Oklahoma City. Second, I am expecting a baby next June. Best wishes, John, Stephanie, and Timothy."

On February 29, 1992, I talked with Stephanie by telephone: John was doing Post Doctorate work at the University of Oklahoma. They may come to Oxford for a few days that summer. John's mother, through their witness, had accepted Christ in Taiwan and planned to come visit them that summer and be baptized. She went on to say, "We appreciate what you have done for us by planting the seed of faith in us."

Their baby girl, Grace, was then twenty-one months old. I thought this was a beautiful example of God's Grace.

At this time in my life I didn't think I would have a grandchild named Grace. Our precious Clara Grace was adopted from China in 2005.

Many international students attend the University of Mississippi. We are able to reach many of these students at church or through these Bible classes. Those that accept Christ as their Savior return to their country, and tell the Good News—that is our mission. The world was coming to us, and we had the opportunity to share the gospel right within our own hometown!

Go into all the world and preach the gospel to every creature.
—Mark 16:15

28

A China Doll for Christmas

I was helping my daughter, Debra, an artist, set up a show at a mall, when two of my friends came by. Debra talked with them a while, and after they left she looked at me and asked, "Did you know that one of those ladies went to China with her son and got a little girl that he and his wife adopted?"

I told her I knew they had been to China, and I even had a photo of their two adopted children. There was a pause in our conversation and I looked at her and said, "Debra, why don't you and John go to China and get you a little girl? I know that Chinese children honor their parents, and she would be a blessing to you as you grow older."

She looked at me and then went on about her work.

That night, when we got back to my house, Debra told her daddy and me to sit down—that she wanted to give us our Christmas present early this year. She handed each of us a small Christmas stocking. I admired it, squeezed it, and then reached inside and pulled out a 5x7-inch picture frame with a baby picture in it. My husband got a different framed picture of the same baby.

Being in the art business, it was not unusual for us to purchase picture frames for each other. I said, "Hey, this is a nice frame, but who is the baby in the picture?"

She looked at me with an expression on her face that I will never forget, and said, "Mother, that is our little girl."

"Oh," I said, "you are going to sponsor a child somewhere?"

"No, Mother, this is our baby girl, and we are going to China to get her in two weeks," she told me with tears in her eyes.

Tears flowed as many questions were asked and answered. How did she keep this adoption process a secret for two long years? We have a wonderful mother-daughter relationship and always share joys and sorrows with each other, but this had been a well-guarded secret.

I still can't believe that I told Debra to go to China to get a little girl. This was very much out of character for me to say this, because I am always concerned when my children travel out of the country.

However, from that night forward, as I looked at the intent, determined, precious little face of that six-month-old baby in the picture, I never had negative thoughts. I had complete peace of mind and wonderful thoughts of being a grandmother, at last, at the age of seventy-two.

As I now look back, I feel the Lord gave me those words at the right time to give Debra and John the parental approval that they desired, and also to reinforce their assurance that this adoption was God's will.

Debra and John were in their mid-forties, had been married eighteen years, and had no children. I had, for the most part, given up on having any grandchildren; however, I still kept my children's books and toys, thinking I might have grandchildren someday.

The decision to adopt all started one day when Debra was at her drawing board, painting, as she often did after teaching school all day. She heard a radio advertisement relating the need for adopting children domestically and internationally. She began to pray about this and began an investigation into various adoption options. She finally told John about her thoughts and prayers.

For the next two years, she completed mountains of paperwork and considered the cost of adoption. At times she became discouraged. Then one day she thought of the money her grandmother had left her. She decided that her grandmother would have been pleased to know that she would invest this money in a priceless child, instead of finishing the basement in their home.

As Debra and John were filling out forms, getting fingerprints, and doing an extensive home study—in the Panlong Village in the Hunan Province of China, a nine-day-old baby was found in a box outside a busy marketplace. On the infant girl was a note, with the exact time and date of her birth, written on a red piece of paper. She was found by a female villager and taken to the QiDong Orphanage after her parents could not be located. The baby was named "Qi FuShan"—Qi, meaning *prayer*, Fu, meaning *blessing* or *happiness*, and Shan, meaning *mountain*.

The long-awaited referral phone call and picture finally came, saying that a little girl was waiting for them in China. Debra and John, along with seven other couples who received referrals from the same Christian adoption service, started their incredible journey to China.

They traveled to Beijing, Changsha, Guangzhou, and saw many amazing sights, such as The Great Wall, Ming Tombs, a cloisonné factory, embroidery factory, the beautiful White Swan Hotel, and much more. The great day came in Changsha, when they arrived at their hotel and saw the babies in the arms of their nannies, waiting for their American parents.

Debra and John recognized their baby—Abbey FuShan Swartzendruber—the determined, but precious face from the picture they had looked at hundreds of times—the baby they had prayed and waited for so long—the baby they had fallen in love with, halfway around the world, was now in their arms at last.

After crying for 30 or 40 minutes for her nanny, she became secure in the arms of her loving mother and daddy. From bus to airplane, stroller to backpack, Abbey FuShan enjoyed the sights and sounds of her native land. She won the hearts of all who saw her. She got hugs and kisses from the street people, as well as clerks and waitresses.

She enjoyed seeing the chickens, ducks, and geese in coops along the streets, fresh fruit and vegetables in the open markets, and snakes, crabs, and lobsters on display for sale in aquariums. She seemed to love every minute of it, taking it all in for the very first time.

Debra and John were so thrilled to see her blossom from the limp baby in a bundle of six heavy layers of clothes, to an active child full of laughter. What a different life she was already experiencing from the life she knew in the orphanage!

The emails and phone calls came often, telling everyone what a beautiful, intelligent, and seemingly perfect eleven-month-old child Abbey was.

It was Christmas Eve 2000, at Grandmother and Granddaddy's house in Oxford, Mississippi, and we were waiting anxiously for our children to come home with their precious "China Doll." Part of the family met them at the Memphis airport with cameras, balloons, and "Welcome Home, Abbey" signs. It was a Christmas we will never forget. Abbey was everything we expected and more. What a Christmas Party we had that night, and from then on it was Christmas everyday!

Amidst the joy and excitement, I could not help but think of another mother who made the ultimate sacrifice in giving up her nine-day-old baby against her will, in order that her lovely, darling daughter would have a better life.

As the children told stories of China on that Christmas Eve, John related an incident that occurred as he and a friend were walking down a street in Changsha. A lady walked up to John and tried to give him her baby girl. She did not understand the adoption process, but she desired a better life for her child. China is filled, not only with millions who long to be free from poverty or the oppressive government, but who are in darkness without Christ. When Abbey was about two years old, her daddy was speaking one night to a group of couples interested in adoption. He mentioned that Abbey probably knew more about Jesus now, at her young age, than most of the people they met on the streets in China.

He told of how Abbey cried the day the nanny handed her to Debra. I could see that Abbey was listening to every word he said, as she sat in Debra's lap. I happened to overhear Abbey as she put her arms around her mother and whispered, "I'm not ever going back to that nanny!"

Abbey FuShan, in her young life, has already touched many lives. She has had a part in influencing couples who have gone to China and returned with their little "China Dolls" that Abbey calls her little sisters.

What a joy to see her at home, singing, drawing, painting, playing little tunes on her violin, and singing "Jesus Loves Me," and doing all the other things an active three-year-old would do.

I know my children did all of this in faith—reaching out for the full measure that God offered them. While other grandmothers were going to their granddaughter's graduations and weddings, I was playing ball with Abbey, making cookies, swinging in the park, having a tea party, and loving every minute of it!

It was certainly God's grace that such a happy, healthy, gifted child was given to us to love—a precious jewel—a gift that keeps on giving.

****

"... The LORD will give grace and glory;
No good thing will He withhold
From those who walk uprightly.
                        —Psalm 84:11

His Grace keeps on giving, because it was in 2005 that Clara Grace Swartzendruber came, also, to fill our hearts and lives. Debra and John thought that Abbey needed a little sister, so they took her with them to her native land, and adopted her twenty-seven-month-old sister, Gracie. They are not sisters by birth, but we knew from the start, God put them together to be "Sisters—by—Heart."

As I write this in 2014, as their grandmother, there is no way I can tell you how much joy these two girls, Abbey, age fourteen, and Gracie, age eleven, have brought to our family. I call them "our little missionaries," because they have gone to hundreds of places, singing and playing their violins. They play and sing for senior groups, weddings, funerals, churches, adoption meetings, schools, and various other concerts. They are both members of local orchestras.

I have no greater joy than to hear that my children walk in truth.   *—3 John 4*

****

When Abbey was two years old, her parents took her to hear "The Singing Christmas Tree" at Bellevue Baptist Church near Memphis, Tennessee. At one point in the program there were children playing the violin. Abbey looked at her mother and said, "That's what I want to do when I grow up."

Soon after this she went to the Oxford Mall with her mother and grandmother. She saw this funny looking man and was told that he was Santa Claus. She had never seen him before and stood at a distance from him. He saw her and said, "What do you want for Christmas, little girl?" She didn't say anything.

He then said, "Do you want a doll?" She shook her head as to say no. He mentioned several more things, to which she shook her head.

Then he said, "Well, what do you want for Christmas?"

She looked at him and said very emphatically, "I want

a violin!"

Well, that told Grandmama and Granddaddy what she wanted. Can you guess what she got for Christmas that year!? At three years old she started taking lessons. God has truly blessed Abbey and Gracie, as they have been a blessing to many people. One of the special songs they sing is "Christmas Wishes," that was written by their mother, Debra Swartzendruber.

Christmas Wishes

1. Adoption is a special word in my family,
I came all the way from China to be 'neath our Christmas tree.
Yes, adoption is a special word in my family.

Chorus: Christmas wishes, yummy dishes, cinnamon and spice
The jingle bells are nice.
I love the tinsel, lights and bows, and even the falling snow,
But my wish for you—to be adopted too!

2. My parents prayed and then obeyed
and when the paperwork was done
It was really very special, 'cause I'm that special one!
Another little baby came a long, long time ago,
The shepherds came, the angels sang,
and His parents loved Him so.
Repeat chorus

3. I'm so very glad my parents came for me.
So I could hear about that wondrous story,
God sent His Son named Jesus on Christmas day you see.
So we could be adopted into His royal family.
Repeat chorus

Spoken tag: If you ask Jesus into your heart.
Sing tag: You'll be adopted too.

Abbey, Gracie, and Grandmama Del.

29

Excerpts From Anson's Journal

My humble beginnings started in a small, but proud, hamlet of Oxford, Mississippi. I was born to Del and Russ Aven, a housewife and a university professor. I led a very happy and carefree life, thanks to the love and caring of my devoted parents. Campus life was wonderful and probably led me to where I am today. The old school yard, tennis camp in the summer, Old Miss baseball games, good friends, and time spent in the Student Union were some of the warmest memories that I treasure. I could fill volumes about any one of these events, but will have to save those stories for later.

My earliest memories come from the spring of 1962. I guess I wasn't quite two years old at the time. A lot of people don't believe this, but I really do have a lot of childhood memories.

Anson, ready for a game of baseball.

It seems like only yesterday, my daddy and I were in the yard throwing the baseball or football, or shooting hoops on the driveway … so many good memories. I pity those who never knew their father, or lost him at an early age, or had a father who never spent time with them. I thank God for fathers who reared their children in a Christian home, who loved them, and provided for them, who spent time with them, and who taught them a lifestyle worth living. When I was a child I assumed my dad was like most dads, but as I grew older I was shocked at how many children never got to experience and enjoy a father like mine.

As a teenager in my church in Oxford, I was involved with a fellowship of friends that met in a building called "The Pines." This group of fellow Christians will always be endeared to me for the love and friendship that was shown through it. Although this building no longer remains, the memories from that "circle" will always be cherished. This group was special, in that even though we had our differences, we also had much in common—the common bond of Jesus Christ. I had three spiritual mentors there. These brothers taught me many lessons in Christian discipleship, but the one I remember the most was that there is strength in Christian groups where each member is sincerely concerned for each other.

Even though that chapter of my life is finished, I can't help but compare that group to my group today—a group that respects each other's differences, but is connected through a common bond. Christians are indeed like a fabric that has been woven from many threads. Each thread is different, but yet forming one interconnected, beautiful tapestry.

As we face tough times, I hope I have the strength and courage to face what lies ahead. God is always shaping our character, as a sculptor chisels a block of stone into a piece of art. We are never to give up on our pursuit of excellence in our careers and lives—God deserves the best, our best.

We wake up, go to work, do some meaningless task that will be forgotten five years from now (in the computer industry, forgotten the next week), come home, prepare dinner, eat, watch TV, and go to bed. Repeat!

What is important in our lives? Is it what we wear to work or how we waste our time waiting for five o'clock? No!! It's the people in our lives and how we make them happy and encourage them. It's the pursuit to live our lives as Christ desires!

****

The doctor said I had myelofibrosis—a rare bone marrow disease and an enlarged spleen—usually found in older people over sixty. When I first learned of my condition and disease, I was devastated. I thought my world was about to end. I have always feared old age and now I may not even have the opportunity. I have exercised all my life, taken few risks, and eaten healthy; rarely ever sick, and never hospitalized. The doctor said the life expectancy, once diagnosed, is three to five years. I can't believe that my parents may outlive me. Even my dogs may outlive me.

Football is a wonderful sport, and so many analogies can be given to real life, I guess it's the hope that I like most. The games that I have seen where a team overcomes incredible odds and claims the victory, this paralleled my life. The odds were against us, but we still had hope that we would win.

I never knew what grandeur existed in the world until my 27th year, when I "came home to a place I had never been before." I have experienced three "births" in my lifetime: a physical birth, a spiritual birth. and an emotional birth. Never before have I been so touched by something in this world, as I was when I first saw the Northern Rockies. I wished at this time I was a poet instead of an engineer. None of my words could describe the beauty and awesomeness of these creations. We were with a church group and first-time skiers. The skiing was fun, but it was only an excuse to be with the mountains.

I have thought a lot about heaven and life after life recently. I realize the promises of Christ—that our life with Him will be so much better than it is here. My limited consciousness can't imagine what it will be like in Heaven. I do know, beyond a shadow of a doubt, that all my needs to be happy will be met.

Lord, I trust You in this part of my life, as I have others. I have moved when You said move, and changed jobs as I was led. So many times I didn't understand why things happened, but can look back on them now and see Your hand at work. Help me to be strong through this and accept that You know how best to use my life. I pray for healing. Thank You for the support of my friends and family. Prayer is our most effective weapon against the harmful things of the world. Amen.

God has blessed my life in so many ways—the best part has been a great family and truly genuine friends.

I read somewhere that once one is diagnosed with a terminal disease, their sympathy toward others' suffering is greatly magnified. I find this to be very true. I tend to become more emotional and empathize more quickly.

What a bad weekend! Why does it always seem to happen like air disasters, in threes? I lost three people this weekend. Three people that I cared for, respected, or held a special place in my life. Why were they all taken this weekend? We'll never know, but I imagine they are all together right now, talking about those they love, seeing those that went before them, and waiting for those yet to come.

In our lives, as it is in nature, the world truly is like a circle, with all things dependent upon each other. Birth, life, death, and new birth are all part of that circle ... that sacred circle. Yes, everything changes, time waits for no man. Time flies like an arrow—straight and true.

I guess I never fully realized that our lives will never remain the same, no matter how much we want them to be; people die, friends leave, and situations change. Many times I have thought about the percentages of death and illness and thanked the Lord that I was in the majority. So many times I have taken for granted health and strength that God had given to me. It's so easy to assume that this will always be with you.

****

Each month when I write out my tithe check, it's an act of faith, because at the end of the month I don't know if I'll have enough money to cover the bills or not. But every month, something comes through, and I make it to the next month.

In my weakness, God's strength is more evident. As I decrease, He increases. He has taught me to rely on Him for all things, and just like He sent manna on a daily basis, He provides for me daily. I will praise Him in the good times and I will praise Him in the storm.

****

While viewing the films of the internal workings of my dad's heart, the cardiologist quoted the statistics and hazards of his condition. If one of the other arteries collapsed, it would be instant death. As I continued to watch the blood and dye flow through the chambers, and course through his veins, I couldn't help but marvel at how wondrously and magnificently we are created; yet, at the same time, how fragile we are. What happens to the years of experience, the knowledge, the emotions that we accumulate in our heart, soul, and mind when we die? I guess I will find out some day.

****

Debra and I sat on each side of her bed, holding her hands, and even though Grandmother never opened her eyes, I knew she knew we were there. About an hour and a half later, I could feel the life leave her body. It was a beautiful experience to hold the hand of someone who is dying ... to be here the moment one of God's saints is called home. I could feel her presence in the room—comfortable, familiar presence that was filled with love. Grandmother had just had her 101st birthday just nine days ago, and now she is gone. One hundred and one years of life, love, experiences, disappointments, exhilarations, friends, family, joys, and sadness.

****

Mt. LeConte, Smoky Mountains—at Easter:

It was a beautiful service that celebrated Good Friday and Jesus' road to the Cross. After each verse was read, a candle would be blown out and then a chorus of "Were you there?" was sung. The room became darker with each candle and lamp extinguished. The wind was gushing and the snow was still falling outside. It was a very beautiful and meaningful service. A service like this means more to me than a hundred services in a million-dollar church. It was simple, sincere, and touching. We broke the homemade bread and drank the wine (grape juice) to celebrate the body and blood of Christ.

It was a perfect morning for the Easter service—very clear and cold. The colors were already forming in the thin clouds that hovered above the mountain ranges. The sunrise that morning was one of the most moving things I have ever seen. The birds were singing happily, the wind was calm, and the sun was slowly appearing over one of the many majestic peaks in the Smokies. "Be still, and know that I am God; ..." (Psalm 46:10). That verse was what I kept hearing over and over that morning. At the end of the service, they released some doves that kept circling the area. It was a beautiful service that only God could prepare.

****

I had a dream of dying. I was suddenly removed from all cares of this world, taken from a cold environ. I could sense the warmth of light. I was engulfed in light. It was liquid light, flowing all around and through me. I wish I had written more of this dream at the time it happened over ten years ago. I still feel the comfort and security of that dream. We understand so much in that netherworld between consciousness and unconsciousness, just after we awake and just before we realize we are back in our physical bodies. Unfortunately, that understanding fades so quickly, we usually don't have time to commit it to our permanent memory, or to write it down. I've had dreams where questions have been answered, only to lose those answers within a few minutes.

****

I've always said that the transition between this life and the next is the greatest adventure. I know now that God is calling me to saddle my horse and travel a new path. But like any explorer, preparation must be first made. Do we have enough food, the right maps, the right equipment, the knowledge to use it, and the right attitude? I feel as though God has given me some time to prepare for this journey and I thank Him for this time. Each day is a gift and I pray that I will use it wisely.

I've made a resolution not to put off important things: letting people know how important they are to me, hugging friends and family every chance I get, expressing gratitude, making others feel good about themselves, and hopefully, providing a legacy through my philosophies that will be passed down to others who knew me.

My philosophy has always been that life is a great adventure, and the friends you meet on that journey are the best part. It is a rare opportunity that one is able to write his own eulogy. I think everyone should take the time to say goodbye to friends and family. We will only be separated for a period of time. I always eagerly anticipated seeing them at holidays, football games, and special events, or just for no reason other than a visit.

God has been gracious in giving me the last seven years, while the doctors said three to five.

I look forward to seeing each and every one of you after a long and happy life here on earth.

My sheep hear My voice, and I know them, and they follow Me.
—John 10:27

Anson's photo of a comet.

Anson Aven's Top Ten Rules for Life

10. Outside is better than inside.
     Watch a sunset daily. Learn nature and see God's miracles.

9.   Always save room for pie.
     Save time to enjoy life.

8.   Leave a place better than you found it.

7.   Watch a Laurel and Hardy or Three Stooges movie as often as possible. My Grandmother Aven, who lived to be 101 years old, taught me this truth—to laugh, love, and live.

6.   Never believe in luck. Always believe in providence.
     God does not play dice with the universe.

5.   Smile.
     People like smiles. I like people that smile and perform random acts of kindness. My Granddaddy Barber was loved by so many people because of his personality and kindness. I can't remember him without a smile on his face.

4.   Love animals.
     To be so smart, man knows so little sometimes. We can learn so much from God's other creations.

3.   "Play when you can. Hunt when you must. Rest in-between." … The Wolf Credo is good enough for me too.

2.   Balance.

1.   The Truth is out there.
     God is the source of all Truth, Peace, and Love.
     Seek God and you will find Truth.

Note: The preceding pages were written by Anson after he was diagnosed with myelofibrosis. This is a small portion of his journal I found after his death.

Photos of Anson.

30

A Sister's Remembrance of Her Brother

I not only learned about hiking from Anson, but also a great deal about our Christian walk through life as well. He taught us how to pack and how to prepare for the hike. Anson taught me, not only to keep my eyes on the destination, but to love the journey. It was always a good experience to go hiking with him, because he made the journey fun!

He showed us how to help fellow hikers along the way. He reached out to help us over creeks and rocks. I have seen my brother race to the top, unload his backpack, and race down to relieve another hiker of their load who might be having trouble. He was always checking on the group to be sure everyone was ok. The Lord wants us to serve others as we walk through life—to help bear one another's burdens, to listen when there is hurt, and be an encourager to those who are discouraged.

Anson was the encourager, with some appropriately-voiced comments that kept me moving.

As you hike the Smoky Mountains, there is a wonderful phenomenon of actually ascending through the clouds. There were two favorite spots Anson liked—Cliff Top and Myrtle Point. We all loved to hike up Cliff Top and see the sunset. Anson really loved waking up early in the morning, before dawn, to reach Myrtle Point. The view was astounding, and the clouds drifted above and below, as you beheld and relished the spectacular beauty of the rising sun in hues of gold and bronze. Such beauty made you forget the aches, pain, and hardships it took to reach that point. Anson loved to sit down on the rocks and drink in the dazzling, breathtaking beauty of the sunrise. It reminded me of a verse in Psalm 30:5 that says, "… Weeping may endure for a night, But joy comes in the morning."

The climb is hard. There are rocky paths and steep inclines. We can slip and have some bad falls in our life. There can be bad weather and storms. There can be aching joints and pain. Anson knew all about these, but he kept following the Trail Guide, our Savior. On May 15, 2007, this Master Trail Guide came down the path and relieved Anson of his load (as Anson had relieved us of our loads so many times). He took Anson by the hand and guided him through the clouds to the summit.

We are a little behind you on the trail, Anson. Thank you for charting for us a good course. You were prepared; you had the courage and endurance to keep going. You helped others along the way and loved the journey. Now all the aches and pains have been forgotten as you are beholding all the beauty, while sitting on the clifftop of Heaven.

Behold, the Lord GOD shall come with a strong hand,
And His arm shall rule for Him;
Behold, His reward is with Him,
And His work before Him.
He will feed His flock like a shepherd;
He will gather the lambs with His arm,
And carry them in His bosom,
And gently lead those who are with young.
Who has measured the waters in the hollow of His hand,
Measured heaven with a span
And calculated the dust of the earth in a measure?
Weighed the mountains in scales
And the hills in a balance?
—Isaiah 40:10-12

Clifftop on Mt. LeConte.

31

Gardenia Story
The Domino Effect

One day I was at Debra's house. She said, "Mama, there is a lady I would like for us to visit. She has cancer and doesn't have long to live. I don't know if she is a Christian or not, and we have been praying for her."

We went to her house and were invited in and went to her bedroom. She was alert and smiling. We talked with her a good while and prayed with her. We came away in peace. Before we left, I was standing by her bed and looked out the window. There was the most beautiful gardenia bush loaded with dozens of white blooms. I told her that gardenias were one of my favorite flowers.

She smiled and said, "When you leave, get you a bouquet of them." I thanked her and we soon left. We picked about a half dozen or more of the beautiful blooms.

We enjoyed the sweet smelling fragrance for several days, even though the blooms had withered. I took them with me when I left my daughter's house. I told her I was going to try to root them, since I didn't have any in my yard.

It was not long until Debra and family were going to this lady's memorial service. The visit with her lingered in my mind and heart as I looked at the plants I had put in water to try to root.

Most of them did root and were placed around my house in various locations. In a few years, there were many blooms on the plants. I began to pick bouquets and take them to neighbors, sick friends, relatives, and anyone who came by my house. I always kept a bouquet on my table for my family to enjoy. I didn't want a bloom to fall to the ground. I rooted many plants that have produced thousands of blooms.

Today, I have about a dozen bushes in my yard. Some of them are probably six feet tall and spread over eight to ten feet in width. I have given away probably hundreds of bouquets and plants rooted in pots. Recently, a bouquet was used in a wedding. One of my friends calls me the "Gardenia lady" when the season comes.

This true story is not told for self praise at all, but as a reminder to me and others of how our actions may reach many people—like the sick lady's bouquet. What we do while living may continue long after we leave this earth. When I was a child, we often played dominoes. Sometimes we would line them up on end and see if we could make them all stand without falling. It was fun to see one touch the other until all had fallen. Our witnessing to one lost soul who becomes a Christian may, by that person, spread to hundreds of other people—the domino effect. I think of the many great preachers of the past, such as Charles Spurgeon, Dwight L. Moody, Mordecai Ham, and today, such as Dr. Billy Graham and Dr. David Jeremiah, who have preached and reached so many people worldwide. Then those people, in turn, reach others with the Gospel of Jesus Christ. May we leave behind the fragrance of a vibrant life that may help transform other lives!

The grass withers, the flower fades,
But the word of our God stands forever.
—Isaiah 40:8

... The harvest truly is plentiful, but the laborers
are few. Therefore pray the Lord of the harvest
to send out laborers into His harvest.
—Matthew 9:37-38

Gardenia bush with lots of blooms.

32

Surveys and Telemarketers

One day I got a call from someone who wanted to know if I would answer a few questions. It was the Health Department. I agreed to answer the best I could.

She asked:

How many people live in your house? "Two."

Are there any under eighteen years? "No, but one acts like it sometimes."

Have you ever smoked? "No ... I take that back, I did smoke a grapevine and some rabbit tobacco one time when I was a child."

Did you ever drink alcohol? "Never ... well, maybe one time back in the 1930s, I drank a swallow or two of muscadine wine; of course, I did drink a lot of "pot liquor" through the years." (For you who may not know, that is turnip green juice.)

Are you diabetic? "No, ma'am, I don't think so."

Have you ever had your sugar level checked? "Yes, my husband says I'm sweet enough."

Do you have a family doctor? "Yes, He is Jesus Christ, the Great Physician."

I mean, do you have a local doctor? "Yes, ma'am, He's about as local as you can get."

Did you ever dip snuff or chew tobacco? "No, the only thing I dipped as a child was cocoa."

In the last month have you had any trouble sleeping? "One or two nights ago I did, and counted sheep, but that didn't help. But since I started doing the Bible verse ABCs, I am asleep long before I get to Zechariah. I start with A—All we like sheep have gone astray. B—Be still, and know that I am God. C—Casting all your care upon Him, for He cares for you, and so on …"

Do you have any anxiety or fear? "Not really, the Lord said fear not, for I am with you."

Do you work? "Yes, ma'am, from daylight to dark."

Do you make more than $25,000/year? "Well, I get a little Social Security check and my retirement check is less than that.

Well, I assume you are retired? "Yes, I try to be. I retire in my lounge chair and take a nap everyday."

Do you have any heart problems? "Not at all, I asked Jesus into my heart when I was thirteen years old, and He has taken care of my heart ever since!"

Well, thank you very much. I think that is all I need to know.

****

I don't like the squirrels to eat the birdseed and drink the hummingbird juice. I don't like the deer to eat my roses. But then I thought—God made them and they are hungry, and these little animals don't know any better.

I get tired of telemarketers and surveys, but I guess they are trying to make a living and put food on their table too, so I thought I would take time to help this lady. Some of this survey is true, but I imagine you have already guessed that some was written for fun. That day my mission field, however, was in my own house as I gave my testimony for Jesus.

Squirrel in the bird feeder.

Hungry deer.

33

A Little More of 'This and That'

I recall a poem I heard one day when I was in college many years ago, and this is my version, which I think is worth repeating.

"What I Like About the South"
It is where the pines grow the highest
and the girls are the shyest,
Where the breeze blows the lightest
and the cotton grows the whitest,
Where the summers are the longest
and the boys are the strongest.

In response to this, I'm thankful that I was born in the South. I like a variety of weather, but wouldn't want to live where there is a lot of cold weather. I have never had to worry about floods or hurricanes in North Mississippi. Yes, we do have tornadoes, but so do many other states.

****

One day a young boy about four years old looked at his mother and said, "Mamma, what are you doing?"

She said, "I'm pulling out the gray hairs on my head."

He looked over at his grandmother, who was sitting nearby, and said, "If Grandmama pulled out all her gray hairs, she would be bald."

****

Through the years I have cut lots of hair. When I tell someone about cutting my husband's hair, they say, "Oh, do you really cut his hair?"

I answer by saying, "Yes, I do—you may not know this, but I was a Barber for twenty-six years." They look at me in question, and say, "I didn't know that!"

"Yes, that's right; I was really a Barber for twenty-six years, and then I married Russ Aven and now I am an Aven," I tell them. They finally start laughing when they get my joke that Barber was my maiden name.

But really, I did cut my grandfather's, my husband's, and my sister's hair, as well as my own for many years.

One day I was at a nursing home and I heard a discussion about one of the older clients that wouldn't let anyone cut his hair. He was really getting wooly. I went over to the man, sat down, and started talking to him. I asked him if he would like for me to cut his hair. He agreed, so I cleared it with the people in charge and went home for my equipment. I came back and gave him a good close haircut. When I finished, the aides and nurses couldn't believe he let me do it, after their unsuccessful efforts. I didn't tell them I was a Barber for twenty-six years!

****

White hair that sheds on a black outfit, or even on a dark color, can really show up! When someone plucks a hair from my back, I can't help but use that as my witness for the day. I say, "Don't we have an awesome, all-knowing God, who even knows the hairs on our head, and even the ones we lose, as the Bible tells us in Matthew 10:30, 'But the very hairs of your head are all numbered'."

****

The following quotes are some things I have heard people say through the years:

- He's as poor as Job's turkey.

- Ya'll come to see us—and set a spell.

- How are you doing? I'm fair to middling.

- The proof is in the pudding.

- You're as slow as Christmas.

- He's as hard-headed as a hickory nut.

- He always got up at the crack of dawn.

- Don't bite off more than you can chew.

- You can lead a mule to water, but you can't make him drink.

- I wouldn't touch that with a ten-foot pole.

- They are dyed in the wool.

- Make hay while the sun shines.

- Don't put all your eggs in one basket.

- Don't count your chickens before they hatch.

- There's something fishy about that.

- You are eatin' like a field hand.

- They want a finger in the pie.

- Great balls of cat fur.

- You're making a mountain out of a molehill.
- I am worn to a frazzle.
- You're off like a jug handle.
- They would wear the horns off a billy goat.
- That is a pain in the neck.
- Prevention is better than pain.
- Being cautious and caring is better than curing.
- No matter how old you are or how old your children are—they are always your children.
- For every child you have—your love is not divided—it is multiplied.
- A family's love makes a house a home—with a mother and a father.

****

Things we didn't have to do when I was a child:
- Pay electric, water, and sewage bills.
- Dry clean clothes.
- Buy gasoline and be concerned about the price.
- Repair washing machines, dryers, refrigerators, cars or trucks, heating and cooling systems, plumbing, and electrical equipment.
- Buy insurance.
- Mow the lawn.
- Rarely went to a doctor or dentist.
- Use sunscreen—a straw hat was good enough.
- No shots before starting to school.
- No garbage or recycle material to deal with.

- Pay income tax, sales tax, property tax, or any other tax.
- Buy batteries for clocks and watches.
- Didn't have to buy meat, milk, eggs, meal, peanuts, vegetables, water, dried fruit, and much more.

****

I remember:

- Penny post cards and 2-cent stamps, also 3-cent stamps for a long time.
- Gasoline from 11 to 17 cents a gallon.
- Some years later, I sold lots of gas at our country store—five gallons for a dollar.
- Bread for 10 cents a loaf.
- We ate cornbread and biscuits, if we had flour.
- Brushing my teeth with soda and salt.
- Our toothbrush was made from a small hickory tree limb.
- We had no Kleenex or paper towels.
- We used salt and flour sacks for handkerchiefs, dishcloths, and some clothes.
- Sears-Roebuck catalogue was for ordering chickens and other items, cutting paper dolls, and starting fires.
- A cast iron was heated on the stove or in the fireplace for ironing clothes.
- Homemade quilts for cover in the wintertime.
- We bought second-hand schoolbooks for ten to twenty-five cents.
- Clothes washed and hung on a barbed wire fence.
- Drinking water from a bucket and dipper.
- Kerosene lamp or lantern for light at night.

I remember eating popcorn from a wire popcorn popper that was held over the fireplace, and eating parched peanuts as we listened to stories that Mother and Daddy would tell us. Some would be Bible stories. Then we would play "She-Come, She-Come," a guessing game of things in the room that started with letters of the alphabet. We also played dominoes and learned a little math as we played. On cold winter days when there was a big snow, Mother would make snow ice cream. It was wonderful, made with snow, milk, sugar, and vanilla flavoring. Ice cream was something we seldom had, because we didn't have electricity, a refrigerator, or even ice.

****

We always enjoyed making sauerkraut. We got fresh cabbage from the garden, cut it into small pieces, sprinkled it with salt, and put it in a churn. We waited for the tangy taste before eating or canning it.

Making butter was another thing we had to do often. It was a tiresome job, especially to a child. The milk was put in a churn, and a wooden dasher or plunger had to go up and down by hand for a long time before the butter formed. Mother put it in a butter mold and pressed all the excess milk out of it. It was delicious with sorghum molasses and cornbread. We drank the buttermilk that was left after the butter was removed.

Sometimes we would go into the woods looking for sassafras trees. They were small trees with different shaped leaves. We would dig up some of the roots and dry them and make sassafras tea. We would boil the roots. Sugar was added to the boiled water for a very tasty tea that we all enjoyed.

****

Games we played when I was a child:

Hop Scotch, Jump Rope. Dodge Ball, Red Light-Green Light, Knock the Tin Can, Follow the Leader, Marbles, Farmers in the Dell, Red Rover, Hide and Seek, Old McDonald Had a Farm, Paper Dolls, London Bridge, Dominoes, and Jacks.

****

When our children were small, we had fun playing the "Knock, Knock" game. Now our joy comes when they come home with their children and "Knock, Knock" on our door. What a joy it is to have the grandchildren come!

****

A merry heart makes a cheerful countenance ...
—Proverbs 15:13

I like to see people smile and hear them laugh. Hopefully, they are happy and enjoying life. I have tried, in this book, to include some of the fun times in my life, also, those of friends and family. I hope it has brought some laughter to you.

With all the sadness, evil, and bad things happening in our world today, I have tried to include stories that would be uplifting. At reunions I love to see and hear a joyous group. People who love the Lord should be the happiest people on earth and enjoying life. I have mentioned several times in these chapters how thankful and blessed I have been to have had Christian parents, grandparents, and family. I can say of them who have gone on to their eternal home that they finished well.

34

God's Communication Lines Are Always Open

It had been a busy week. My daughter, Debra, and two grandchildren had been here shopping and working on various projects. Abbey, my thirteen-year-old computer helper, told me it was not working. She could not get on the internet. She used it often in her school and church work.

I called the internet company and got a kind and helpful man who spent a long time checking various causes for the problem. I finally let Abbey work with him on it because she knew more about it than I did.

Finally, he said my modem was six years old and needed to be replaced. He said he would ship one to me the next day. I got it and wasn't sure I could install it, so I put it aside until I could get someone to help me. I soon needed to read my e-mail and look up some information.

I went to the computer and looked at the ball of wires connecting it to the modem and three printers. I got down on my knees and had to crawl under the table to see if, by chance, anything was disconnected. I didn't find any problems, but I did unplug and replace several wires. I have knee problems and seldom get on my knees, because it is hard to get up.

I was getting tired and about ready to call it quits when I

thought, *Here I am on my hands and knees, at eighty-four years old, trying to fix this problem on my own. I haven't even asked God to help me!* Since I was on my knees, I thought this was no better time than to pause and ask God to fix my computer and help me get out from under the table. This is what I did.

I crawled out and back into my chair by His help. I got my composure and turned on the computer and waited. It came on as clear as it had always been! I stopped and thanked the Lord. I should have prayed before I went to all this trouble.

Many of my prayers have not been answered that soon. Sometimes they were not answered in the way I asked, and I found out later it was a blessing they weren't. As is often said, God sometimes says no, or wait a while.

In Jeremiah 33:3 the Scripture says, "Call to Me, and I will answer you, and show you great and mighty things, which you do not know." In 1 Peter 5:7 it says, "casting all your care upon Him, for He cares for you," and Matthew 7:7 says, "Ask, and it will be given to you; seek, and you will find; knock, and it will be opened to you."

I often ask the Lord to help me find things I have lost or misplaced in the house. Many times my prayers are answered and sometimes the answer is, wait a while. Sometimes while I am waiting and looking, I find something I needed worse than the other item.

I know these are little insignificant things. There are much more important prayers to be said, for the unsaved, sickness, jobs, financial, and other problems that we need to pray and cry out to the Lord to answer.

I believe in praying. It is hard to think about people who are lost, without Jesus. How do they cope with tragedies in their lives? The first thing most Christians do when bad things happen is to fall to their knees and ask God for His mercy and grace.

Aren't we glad our communication with Him is always

available—not like the telephone or internet? He hears our pleas when we call out to Him. He never slumbers nor sleeps. What an awesome God we have who even knows the hairs on our head and every sparrow that falls to the ground. We are blessed! He loves us and cares about our every need! Praise the Lord! Amen.

I love the LORD, because He has heard
My voice and my supplications.
Because He has inclined His ear to me,
Therefore I will call upon Him as long as I live.
                                        —Psalm 116:1-2

35

What If? ...
Gracie Swartzendruber's Testimony

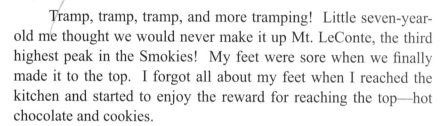

Tramp, tramp, tramp, and more tramping! Little seven-year-old me thought we would never make it up Mt. LeConte, the third highest peak in the Smokies! My feet were sore when we finally made it to the top. I forgot all about my feet when I reached the kitchen and started to enjoy the reward for reaching the top—hot chocolate and cookies.

We signed in at the main lodge and then we went to our usual cabin to unpack. I was really glad to hear the supper bell ringing. Supper always brings good solid food to our starving stomachs. Even though it's always the same menu each year, it's the most delicious food you've ever put in your mouth, because hiking makes you really hungry.

After supper we took another hike up to Cliff Top to see the sunset. It is very beautiful on top of the mountain. You can see a long way, with many mountains in the distance. The wind is always blowing; Mommy's curls were blowing ferociously! You are surrounded by clouds and the drop-off is very scary. I began to wonder where I would go if I fell off that cliff!

When we hiked down, I was very tired and ready to go to bed that night. But as I was getting out of my hiking shoes, I pondered over the thought of what if I should die up here on this mountain; what if I were to die tonight? Where would I go? I jumped into bed and I guess I did go to sleep, but later that night I woke up. Everyone was asleep except me. I finally went back to sleep, but I had three very disturbing dreams. In my dream there was a tornado, a forest fire, and a hurricane, and each disaster played its course very nicely, and all of them killed me! I went to the judgment seat of God and was sentenced to go to hell, but at that point I woke up. I got out of bed, put on my socks and shoes, and tiptoed out the door. I walked down the rock path to the dining lodge and sat down on the top step to wait for the breakfast bell.

By the time the bell rang, my family had gathered, along with all the other campers; and we entered the dining lodge to feast on pancakes, scrambled eggs, homemade biscuits, and apple butter. Throughout this delicious meal, however, I could not keep still for long and I ate very little. I leaned over and whispered in Daddy's ear that I needed to have him come outside with me. When we were alone, I told my daddy that I wanted Jesus to be the King of my life. I could see the happiness on his face.

We hiked down the mountain, finished our Gatlinburg trip, and returned home. It was late when we got back, so we unpacked the car and I went to bed. That night I had another dream, but it was splendid! In the dream, it was the tornado that killed me, but this time I went to Heaven. It was wonderful!

It took about a year before I decided to walk to the front of the church to tell Brother Wes and everyone about my decision to follow Jesus. It was April 17, 2011, right before we were to take our trip back to Mt. LeConte, when I walked down the aisle. I was the last person to make a decision for Jesus in our church, because on April 27, 2011, a tornado came and took our town and church away. Our house was left, and a few months later, a temporary church was built. I was the last person to walk down the aisle before the tornado, but I was the first person to be baptized in our temporary church. Another one of my friends was baptized too, and her name is Gracie, just like me! That Sunday we were not baptized in a baptistery or in a creek, but in a crystal clear swimming pool! What if you died in a tornado, or in a hurricane, or even on a sinking ship like the Titanic; where would you go? I'm happy I'm on my way to Heaven!

****

Sometime before Gracie was to be baptized, she came to me one day real depressed, and looked as if she might start crying. I put my arms around her and asked her what was wrong. She said in a very somber voice, "Grandmama, I know I have Jesus in my heart, but I just don't know about getting baptized."

I questioned her about her thoughts and we discussed the meaning of baptism. A few days later she told her mother that she thought she would just find an old-timey Methodist Church and get sprinkled!

In the meantime, their church was destroyed in a tornado. They got permission to use a swimming pool for the baptismal service. It was raining the day of the service. They had to walk from their temporary church building in the rain to the swimming pool.

It was a very blessed service, and all went well with Gracie as she was baptized. When I saw her the next time, I told her I thought about her that day because she got her wish—that is, she got sprinkled on the way to get baptized!

Bro. Wes White baptizing Gracie in the swimming pool.

Photos of Gracie hiking Mt. LeConte.

36

Twice Blessed
by Abbey Swartzendruber

Fourteen years ago in a small town in China, a little girl that was nine days old was left beside a marketplace. Her birthmother hoped that someone would find her baby and would take care of her. A woman did find the baby and took her to a nearby orphanage, and there the child would live for the next few months. When the baby was 11 months old, something very special happened to her. She was adopted!! That baby was me! When the Lord spoke to my parents and told them to adopt a little girl, they obeyed. Because they heard the voice of the Lord and obeyed, I was given a family, a chance to learn, grow, and thrive, but best of all I came to a saving knowledge of Jesus. Even before I started talking, my mama and daddy taught me about how much Jesus loves me. How He came to the earth as a baby, lived, and then died on a cross—just for me! How He took the punishment for our sins.

When I was two years old, I asked for a violin and received one that Christmas. I started violin lessons the very next year and have been playing ever since. My desire was to bring joy to others through my music and give the glory to the One who gave me the ability to play. As I look back, I wonder what life would have been like if I had not been adopted. Most likely I would have been on my own to find food or means of survival. There would have been no opportunity for an education and no chance of my learning to play the violin. Perhaps I would be working in the rice fields. One thing remains certain—I would never have heard the name of Jesus and become a Christian. I am so thankful that God touched the hearts of my parents and placed me into a wonderful Christian home. Just as my parents adopted me, I was also adopted into God's family. I have become twice adopted. What a blessing that is!

37

Lost and Found
Toto and the Tornado
by
Debra Aven Swartzendruber

The tornado ripped through the small town, damaging buildings and injuring people. A short time later, an unusual thing happened.

My daddy was out in the backyard one morning, putting birdseed in the feeder. To his surprise, when he looked down, he saw a little puppy. The puppy followed him to the carport and my mother said, "Now, where in the world did a cute little thing like this come from; I wonder what kind of dog it is?"

The next day one of her questions was answered when the meter man came to read the meter and saw the little dog, who had taken up residence in the carport. He told my mother, "Ma'am, that little dog is someone's baby. It's a Yorkshire terrier, and they are real expensive dogs. Somebody's crying over losing that dog."

Mother fed and watered the little dog. It was a concern to her that "Toto," the nickname she had given him, was someone's pet, and upon closer examination, the little Yorkie looked as if he had a big gash in his back. She called and searched and basically exhausted every avenue of finding the owner of Toto. My mother and I call each other everyday, and it was quite a surprise for me to hear the story of the strange appearance of this little dog!

Toto had to have stitches in his back and the vet recommended some shots, since the origin was unknown. When my daughters came to visit their grandmama, they fell in love with Toto!! The time came to go home, and my daughters bundled up Toto and brought him home with us, but their daddy was not as enthusiastic about this little vagabond! He said, "That dog is someone's pet, ya'll need to take him back right now!"

With two weeping little girls, back went Toto. That night, Abbey, my oldest, was heartbroken and said, "Mama, I wanted to keep Toto."

I knew she had her heart set on having a Yorkie, and Toto had won her heart; it was with a heavy heart myself that I told both my girls, "Well, your daddy is right, this little dog belongs to someone and they are very sad because their little baby is lost. What we need to do right now is pray. We need to pray that we are able to find Toto's owner because that is the right thing to do."

Abbey replied, "I know it's the right thing to do, but we will never be able to have an expensive little dog like Toto; we will never be able to afford one."

It was hard, but we prayed. The next day was my birthday and we all went out to eat and celebrate. When we walked up to the restaurant's front door, Abbey and I stood in shock, as both of us noticed the poster up in the window. It was a photograph of a little Yorkie that looked regal with an exquisite miniature crown on its head. Underneath the photograph were these words, "LOST DOG, REWARD. IF FOUND, CALL ..." and the phone number to call was listed. Abbey looked at me with an expression of horror and hurt on her face and said, "That's not our dog, that's not Toto!"

After a span of silence, I replied, "It may not be, honey, but we have to call anyway." I fumbled for a scrap of paper to copy the number down.

When we got back to my dad and mom's home, we made the phone call. The nice lady answered a few questions. Then finally, I asked, "What was the color of your dog's collar?"

She replied, "Red." I knew at this point that Toto was indeed her dog. I had a reluctant feeling of joy for this nice lady whose pet had been found. I knew that Toto was really not ours, and I had done the right thing; but at the same time, I still felt such a sense of loss, and I was especially hurt for the sake of my daughters. They had fallen in love with this little two-pound ball of fur!

I said, "I believe I have your dog."

On the other end I could hear weeping, and through the lady's tears she sobbed out, "My home was destroyed by the tornado and I lost everything, except for my life and my dogs. You see, I live alone and they are my babies!"

I gave her directions to get to our house and she cried, "I'll be there in five minutes." We were standing out in the yard when she drove up. Abbey was holding Toto, and when the lady saw her dog, she began to weep and scooped him up into her arms. It was such a happy reunion between dog and owner. Toto was indeed her dog from all the kisses he gave her! The lady was still crying happy tears when she said, "I thought I would never see my baby again; I had almost given up hope."

She told us an amazing story of how her home was destroyed by the recent tornado, how she had just gotten out of the hospital, how she and her dogs (three Yorkies) were living in a temporary condo, and how this little fellow was hit by a car, and then picked up by the ones who had run over him. Evidently, the one who hit the little dog released him on the highway near my mom and dad's home, and he walked all the way to their neighborhood, seeking help. We had a good visit, and when the time came to say goodbye to our newfound friend and to Toto, the nice lady looked at Abbey and said, "My dear, because you were honest and helped me to find my baby, I would like to do something for you."

I knew Abbey and Gracie's hearts were breaking. They had fallen in love with Toto, and it was so hard to say goodbye, but Abbey smiled and looked up at the nice lady, wondering how she might show her appreciation. She would probably give them some money, or candy, or some such thing as a reward. I could see that Abbey was bracing herself to be polite and thank the lady, no matter what was given. The lady bent down and looked into Abbey's eyes, and said, "My little female Yorkie is about to have puppies, and you can have the pick of the litter."

Abbey and Gracie looked at each other and started jumping up and down, dancing and laughing! The dream that Abbey felt would never happen was coming true—a purebred, and yes, very expensive little Yorkie would be hers!

It was an exciting day when the puppies were born! Abbey's pick of the litter turned out to be a sweet little female! Many years have passed since we adopted this little Yorkie into our family and home. What a blessing little "Mei Mei" (which means "Little Sister" in Chinese) has been! Abbey and Gracie have enjoyed taking Mei Mei on walks, fixing her hair in a ponytail on top of her head, and teaching her tricks. Gracie actually talks to this little dog as if she is a real person, dresses her in doll clothes, and plays with her as if she is another child!

There have been a few times in my life that God answered our prayers in miraculous ways, and I consider this event one of those times. A merciful God answered our prayer, even though it was a hard prayer to pray. We prayed in faith that He would help us find the owner of Toto, and He did. A gracious God then gave Abbey and Gracie the desires of their hearts—a beautiful little Yorkie puppy of their very own! We, as parents, want to give good things to our children, and oh, how God wants to bless and give good things to us, His children—we who believe! I have learned that God's power is released only when I prayerfully trust and obey, as the old song says.

But seek first the kingdom of God and His righteousness, and all these things shall be added to you.   —Matthew 6:33

Abbey, dressed as Dorothy in the Wizard of Oz, with Mei Mei in the basket.

38

Dead or Alive?

by

Debra Aven Swartzendruber

(written about her great-great-grandfather)

Amos Wesley Aven
December 25, 1844–September 30, 1931

For now we see in a mirror, dimly, but then face to face. Now I know in part, but then I shall know just as I also am known.
—1 Corinthians 13:12

History is a favorite subject of mine. Here in the South, our history has been passed down one story at a time, told and re-told to our children, and their children, and their children's children. Such is the case of this story that I am about to relate to you. My grandmother would settle down in her favorite chair, after a good meal or a tea time with refreshments, and giggle just a little; then she would look at me and smile, and I knew a good story was on the way. She would point her finger at me and good-naturedly say, "During the War Between the States, your great-great-granddaddy fought for General Robert E. Lee."

Grandmother Aven.

She continued to relate the fact that Amos Wesley Aven, my great-great-grandfather, was just a young boy of seventeen when he decided to join the army of Northern Virginia. As a child I marveled over the fact that he fought in the Civil War. "Wes" joined a group of young men in Yalobusha County, Mississippi, known as the "Dixie Boys" (Company D 48th Mississippi Infantry CSA). This group of men walked all the way to Virginia to join General Lee's 2nd Battalion.

The 48th Mississippi Infantry saw many battles and endured heavy fighting. Wes was a part of each of these battles, and in fact, at one time, was a prisoner of war. On May 5, 1864, there was one particular battle in which his Company fought gallantly and had actually captured 150 prisoners. During this battle, known as The Battle of the Wilderness, there was much loss and injury within the ranks. On this fateful day, however, Wes suffered a great tragedy. He was shot in the head.

My eyes, as a child, really got big when my grandmother related to me the next sequence of events. There was no telephone, texting, or internet at this time and news traveled slowly. The family received the news that Wes had been shot. They presumed their son was dead. I cannot imagine how his poor mother grieved. Times were hard here in the South, sons were necessary to help manage and take care of the farm. The family had no way of knowing that Wes had been taken to a hospital in Virginia. A doctor, however, with the rudimentary medical knowledge of the time, took a silver dollar, placed it over the hole in Wes's head, and sewed it up.

Wes healed and rejoined the army, serving until the very end. He and his fellow "Dixie Boys" were a sparse remnant, as General Lee and his army laid down their arms during the surrender at Appomattox on April 12, 1865.

During his service in the army, Wes suffered pain, injury, starvation, thirst, loss of friends and loved ones, and loss of property. He was mustered out of the army and was given a shirt, a pair of pants, and some shoes. He was also given $10.00 to help him get back home to Mississippi. By this time, Wes was twenty-one years old, and it took him two years to walk home. It had been three to four years since his mother, father, and brothers had heard he had been shot.

After the war here in the South, it was common to see men making their way home. One day Amos Wesley's mother, Mary, was on the front porch shelling peas. She glanced up. Down the road, she saw someone coming. This man was different, however, from all the others she had seen in passing. She said, "That looks like Wes!" She squinted her eyes and thought, "That walks like Wes!" Her surprise turned to fear as she thought it might be a ghost! But as he drew closer, she could see it was indeed her son, Amos

Wesley, in the flesh. She threw the peas up in the air, and began to run down the road to meet her son that she had believed was dead! Many of us here in the South shout when there is something to shout about, and I'm sure there was shouting from his mother as she ran down that road to meet her son! I can imagine Chesley, his father, and his brothers running to meet him, and all the hugging and crying for joy that went on that day! What a day of rejoicing. A son who was thought to be dead was now actually alive!

Traditions are good, especially those traditions of sitting around the dinner table, telling family stories. Children love to hear stories told by their grandparents. I know that my girls beg, "Please tell us a story of when you were young, Granddaddy—please tell us about your childhood, Grandmama!" I'm glad my grandmother took the time to tell me the stories of our family. These stories shaped my life and gave me a sense of place and heritage. She would throw back her head and laugh at what Wes always told to his children and grandchildren, referring to the silver dollar that was permanently covering the hole in his head, "I'll never be without money, and I'll never die broke!"

(Left) Amos Wesley Aven. (Right) Amos with two of his daughters.

The account of my great-great-grandfather can be compared to our Christian walk here in this world. Just like Wes, we are in a hostile environment, fighting a battle and struggling to reach our home. The world has proclaimed that our God is dead. The world also looks at believers as foolish and weak. The culture tells Christians that the moral battles we fight are fruitless and unnecessary.

To live the Christian life is hard. We fight many spiritual battles, and sometimes we feel like we have lost the war. Here in America, Christians are pummeled in the media, mocked at school or the workplace, and in some cases, have even lost their jobs because of their faith. We sometimes feel like laying down our arms to fight no more. The battle for many Christians in other countries includes being persecuted, put in prison, and sadly, some are even put to death. Many of us feel downtrodden and oppressed.

The Lord promises us, however, that if we trust in Him, obey His commandments, and remain faithful in the fight, that we will see Him one day and receive the reward that is laid up for us.

Fight the good fight of faith, lay hold on eternal life, to which you were also called and have confessed the good confession in the presence of many witnesses.   —1 Timothy 6:12

Today, we cannot see Jesus, nor can we touch Jesus, but we know from historical and biblical accounts that there were eyewitnesses to His death, burial, and glorious resurrection. Many saw Him alive, even after He was known to be dead!

"Behold My hands and My feet, that it is I Myself. Handle Me and see, for a spirit does not have flesh and bones as you see I have."   —Luke 24:39

We know that He is working in the lives of those who love and obey Him, from the many testimonies that have been recorded of the past and present heroes of the faith. Finally, we see His presence in our lives if we faithfully seek Him. But one day, my dear Christian, you will look up and see the One you love, the One who died for you providing eternal life; you will see Jesus coming. If you are shelling peas, you will throw them down. In fact, all your work in this world will stop. You will start running toward Him, and then you will be home forevermore, dear one! What a glorious day!

I am He who lives, and was dead, and behold, I am alive forevermore. Amen. ...   *—Revelation 1:18a*

39

Happy Parents, Happy Children

by

Debra Aven Swartzendruber

"After all," Anne had said to Marilla once, "I believe the nicest and sweetest days are not those on which anything splendid or wonderful or exciting happens but just those that bring little pleasures, following one another softly, like pearls slipping off a string." —From *Anne of Avonlea*, L. M. Montgomery

After much thought and deliberation, and after living many years and being involved with many endeavors, after living eighteen years of married life without children, and then living the past twelve years of that married life with children, I have come to the conclusion and the profound realization that the greatest blessing in this life is the joy of a happy and peaceful home!

The screen door slammed behind me. In my memory, I can vividly hear the little tapping of the dangling hook. Part of my childhood was an endless summer, spent with my brother. We stayed outside until dusk nearly every day, breathing in the humid Mississippi air, catching lizards, frogs, and lightening bugs. We feasted on watermelon, corn on the cob, and fried okra. We built grand fortresses for kings or dug foxholes in wet sand for my brother's G. I. Joes. We held powwows in a handmade teepee one day, and on another afternoon, the cowboys fought fierce battles with arrows flying and cap pistols smoking.

(Left) Debra and Anson with chickens.

(Right) Debra and Anson enjoying a sack race.

When we weren't actually participating in our imaginary adventures, we were reading the stacks of books checked out of the public library. Our public library was in the Courthouse, which was in the middle of town on the square. As I recall those days, it brings a sort of comfort as I remember climbing those well-worn steps, opening the creaking door, and seeing the shelves and shelves of books. Just the feel of the bindings and the smell of the pages would elate my young heart, as I pulled authors such as Robert Zim, Barbara Clooney, Dr. Seuss, and Garth Williams from the shelves. We carried stacks and stacks of books home, and I remember many a happy afternoon spent under a shade tree, drinking in the words and illustrations of those written treasures.

My brother, Anson, and I also played lots of games such as chess, checkers, Monopoly, and Rook. Anson loved electronics and learned Morse code. He built radios and was into astronomy. I was more the artist, painter, and had a bent toward biology. Between us we created periscopes, walkie-talkies, can and string telephones, and Rube Goldberg contraptions. Anson had all manner of wires strung up in his room, along with a stamp collection, and the latest baseball cards.

Early on, Anson was practicing his skills to be an electrical engineer.

I had jars of bugs, shelves with blue jay feathers, a rock collection, art pads full of drawings, and articles about outer space. We loved music, all kinds of music—classical, bluegrass, Southern gospel, hymns, ragtime, old-time calliope, Irish, and so forth.

I really thought we were pretty normal kids, doing pretty

normal things. But looking back on our lives, I can see something that is pretty spectacular and unusual in our culture today—our parents gave us one of the greatest gifts that parents can give their children—a happy childhood. In examining what they did to insure that my brother and I not only grew up as happy kids, but as responsible adults, I began to delve into their methods of rearing us. These are the points that I have discovered that may help younger, struggling parents, and even to see how I can better raise my two girls.

How My Parents Gave Us a Happy Childhood

We always ate together when we were at home. Our mother made us a lunch to take to school. During the summer months, we ate nearly every meal together. Our dad was at work during the noon meal, but we ate breakfast and supper together. Many times we ate meals with our grandparents and aunt, who lived next door. Mornings were wonderful! Anson and I woke up to the smell of bacon frying. Our mom made homemade biscuits adorned with Blackburn syrup. We usually had scrambled eggs, some type of fruit, orange juice, and milk. In the summer, our noon meal consisted of fresh vegetables from the garden, such as peas, corn, okra, squash, green beans, tomatoes, radishes, and potatoes. The night meal or "supper" was vegetables and maybe some meat, like chicken, or a hamburger patty, or in the winter months, vegetable soup.

Our parents read to us. Bedtime at our household was great. Mom and Dad took turns reading to us. Mom also read to us during the day and this made our imaginations soar, plus it gave us a love for literature.

We had schedules and boundaries. We had set times to go to bed, do homework, practice, and eat. There were rules. We learned what was expected of us and how to respect our mom and dad.

Our parents and grandparents took the time to play. Our dad played tennis, baseball, basketball, softball, and ping pong with us. Our mom entered our world by introducing us to jacks, the washer game, horseshoes, and "She-Come, She-Come." Our grandparents enjoyed playing Rook, Monopoly, Scrabble, and other games which we loved.

We lived close to our grandparents, aunts, uncles, and cousins. Anson and I had four grandparents who loved us dearly, and we gained from their wisdom. They told us stories and gardened with us. Our paternal grandmother and maternal granny would sew for us. They would make us pies, cakes, cookies, and other goodies. Our Granddaddy Aven brought us a little bag of candy every time he came to visit us. I will never forget the peanut butter logs and other confectionary treasures held within that little brown bag. When we visited him in Water Valley, we would walk to the store where he worked as a meat butcher, and he would reward us with some candy at the store. Our Granddaddy Barber told us stories of the days when he was sheriff, and he and Anson grew big gourds, pumpkins, and other vegetables. We helped him dig potatoes, gather tomatoes, pick and shuck corn, and even sell the extra produce! He always told us, "Do what is right, even if it takes the skin off!"

Our parents and grandparents gave us a sense of place and time in history. From the time we were very small children, they would tell us stories about when they were small. They would also pass down stories they had heard from their parents and grandparents, giving us accounts that dated back to the War Between the States, and even back to the Revolutionary War and founding of America. This gave us an appreciation of history in a more personal way.

Our parents taught us that our love for Jesus and our relationship with Him were the most important things in our lives. They made sure we knew God's commandments. They let us know that we were not perfect; but they gave us mercy and grace when we made mistakes, which in turn helped us to learn from those mistakes. And they introduced us to a Savior who forgives sins when we truly repent or turn from those past wrongs. They lived the principle that when we are in obedience to God, then all other relationships are in harmony (including obedience to our parents). In fact, I can look back on their example of obedience being more important than sacrifice. I will never forget my dad having his quiet time with the Lord, studying his Bible, and then kneeling beside his bed to pray. Both my mom and dad were prayer warriors and they taught us to pray. They took us to church whether we wanted to go or not. As long as I can remember, my mom and dad have served in the church in leadership positions. I helped my mom with the four-year-old Sunday school department. Then when I got older, I began to teach the fifth and sixth graders and help with the youth.

The example of humble obedience to the Lord that our parents lived out in front of us caused us to know what real commitment looked like. It was not always their purpose to make us "happy" in every circumstance, but instead, to shape our character. They are passing on a Christian heritage for their children as well as grandchildren.

Our parents laughed with us. They laughed with us often. Shinichi Suzuki has a famous saying, paraphrased "Smiling parents have smiling children." As far back as I can remember, both sets of my grandparents, and my parents, laughed. They played good-natured jokes, told funny stories, and as they would relate current happenings to us, they would find some measure of humor in each event. As a result of not taking life too seriously—we learned to laugh at ourselves.

We did not go on elaborate vacations, nor did we have many worldly or material goods, yet our parents blessed us with what the word "Home" actually meant. The very mention of the term "Home" brings warmth and comfort to me. What I have described in this book are those incredibly simple, everyday kinds of days— simple and yet exquisite pearls, in a legacy that our parents passed on to us, and that we, in turn, can pass down to our children.

*(Above) Anson with Joy.
(Right) Sunflower garden,
with Anson on a tall
ladder. (Below) Happy
parents, happy children.*

40

Old Age

I am as old as Shirley Temple, Mickey Mouse, and Dubble Bubble. Now you know how old I am!

At what age do you think you are old? I am thankful for every birthday I have had and glad I have not been denied the privilege of having them. I count every year a gift from God and thank Him for it.

Our senior adult group at church is called "The XYZ Group." Some thought, since this was the last of the alphabet, it was inferring that our group was on its way out. Also, their theme song is "I'll Fly Away." Everyone soon learned that the XYZ really meant "Xtra (Extra) Years of Zest." They are a

Del playing tennis with Gracie.

wonderful, active group, who love the Lord, and meet each month to have a meal and a time of fellowship. They travel and enjoy many things together.

Another church group was, by mistake, called "Over the Hill Group." They soon learned of their mistake. Their name was "The Hill Toppers." They had attained the hilltop of life, bearing fruit, serving, and abiding in Christ. Another senior adult group is known as the BALL, which stands for "Be Active, Live Longer."

The Psalmist portrays the fruitfulness of those who love God in old age:

> *The righteous shall flourish like a palm tree,*
> *He shall grow like a cedar in Lebanon.*
> *Those who are planted in the house of the LORD*
> *Shall flourish in the courts of our God.*
> *They shall still bear fruit in old age;*
> *They shall be fresh and flourishing,*
> *—Psalm 92:12-14*

One translation says, "They will stay fresh and green," while another says, "They shall be fat and flourishing." Now, which one do you prefer?

Many times we have heard it's not the number of days we have left that is the most important, but how we use the days the Lord has given us.

Proverbs 20:29 says, "… the splendor of old men is their gray head." I received my gray hair when I was very young and began to put black color on my gray curls that were once black. That was a chore for me, so I decided if the splendor of old men was their gray head, then maybe this would apply to women also. I certainly didn't want to miss any of my "splendor;" therefore, I have been gray ever since.

I was thirty-one years old when my son was born, and my hair was about half-gray then. I wondered if I would be asked if this baby was my grandchild—no one did, however.

The thing that concerns me most about old age is that I'm not able to do all the things I once did and still like to do. A great percentage of folks in their seventies and eighties, and some well into their nineties, can still serve the Lord in many ways.

Moses was eighty years old when God told him to lead the Israelites on their historic journey across the Red Sea into the Promised Land. After forty years in the wilderness, Moses went up on Mount Nebo where he could view the land that the Lord had given His people. It was here that he died at the age of one hundred and twenty.

My sister's first grade schoolteacher at O'Tuckolofa School was Miss Theora Hamblett. She had to stop teaching that year because of ill health. She started painting when she was fifty-five years old and became a well-known artist. She painted many pictures until her death at age eighty-two.

Ronald Reagan was in his late seventies at the end of his second term as President.

While in Vermont one year, I visited the Grandma Moses Schoolhouse and Bennington Museum. The largest collection of Grandma Moses's paintings is displayed here, along with her first painting. At seventy-six years of age, she had arthritis in her hands, and had to give up embroidering, and started painting. She couldn't hold a needle, but she could hold a paintbrush. She painted over a thousand pictures from seventy-six years until her death at one hundred and one.

Benjamin Franklin was an inventor and was one of the Founding Fathers of the United States when he was in his seventies and eighties. A reminder of his life is still with us today on the one hundred dollar bill.

I say all this to show that many people lead very productive lives late in life.

Many years ago, Edward Everett Hale said, "I am only one, but I am one. I cannot do everything, but I can do something. And I will not let what I cannot do interfere with what I can do." One of my Sunday school teachers often quoted this to her class. She changed the last sentence to read, "And what I can do, by the grace of God, I will do."

As I grow older, the more I realize how much my personal family, church family, and Sunday school class mean to me. To have a place to worship and serve the Lord has been such a blessing through the years.

In the fifty-seven years I have been a member of the First Baptist Church in Oxford, Mississippi, I have been blessed with eight pastors and several dedicated Sunday school teachers. During these years I served in various areas, including the media center, youth activities, Vacation Bible School, and as a teacher for the preschool department for seven years. It was such a joy to watch these young children grow in their love for Jesus.

My present Sunday school class is known as the "Friendship Class," and they have indeed lived up to this name! There has been

Friendship Sunday School Class.

such a bond of love within this class of precious ladies. Many are widows and live alone, but they would be quick to tell you that they do not really live alone---God is always with them! This senior group, however, is a gathering of ladies with a mission. They are involved in community services, provide food and transportation when needed, they are prayer warriors, active in passing out tracts, and speaking forth the Word of God to the lost. One special mission project each month is giving money to provide clean water in countries where it is needed.

When troubles, loss, or any other need arises, the phones belonging to these ladies start ringing. Their help, along with that of other church members, is dependable. Friends who share burdens, sorrows, happiness, encouragement, and the Word of the Lord with others are friends indeed.

We don't know when a Christian's last chapter will be written, but we all want to finish well. We want to leave a legacy for our children and grandchildren. Memories of loved ones who have gone to be with the Lord linger long after they are gone. I often encourage some of my contemporaries to keep a journal and write their autobiography. Our words written today may be a blessing to those who read them in years to come. I have kept a journal for the last forty-five years. I regret I didn't keep one during my children's first years of life. I look back through some of my journals and read where many prayers were answered and how God blessed our lives.

If we live well now, we will, no doubt, finish well. Today is the only day we have, yesterday is gone, and tomorrow may not come. As I have often said, "You don't have to be old to die." How many people miss old age? They are taken before they reach it. All we have to do is read the daily paper and see the young people whose lives have been cut short.

We were not created to live forever on this earth, but we are promised eternal life forever if we have Jesus Christ as our Lord and Savior.

... My grace is sufficient for you,
for My strength is made perfect in weakness.
                              —2 Corinthians 12:9

But as it is written:

"... Eye has not seen, nor ear heard,
Nor have entered into the heart of man
The things which God has prepared for those who love Him."
                              —1 Corinthians 2:9

The LORD has done great things for us,
And we are glad.
                              —Psalm 126:3

We can live in splendor!

Current photo of Russ and Del.

41

Just Give Me a Little More Time, Lord

by Del Aven (April 2002)

Just give me a little more time, Lord—
There's so much I want to get done
today before the setting of the sun.
Make my day just a little longer,
and make my body a whole lot stronger.

Make my day a little longer, Lord—
A friend needs my help,
Lord, guide my every step.
Many have burdens to bear—
it's Jesus, I want to share.

Just give me a little more time, Lord—
To let others know someone cares,
and that they are always in my prayers.
To those worried, in pain and tears,
help me, Lord, to calm their fears

Make my day a little longer, Lord—
Strengthen my faith and make me strong
to love and help guide those who do wrong.
May their life be turned around,
so their name in "The Book of Life" be found.

Just give me a little more time, Lord—
May I keep my priorities right today,
and don't let things get in my way.
I do not know today what I will face,
but sufficient will be Your wonderful Grace.

Make my day a little longer, Lord—
May I be a better sister, mother, and wife,
and may I truly live the Christian life—
So my grandchildren will see
the grown-up person they would like to be.

Just give me a little more time, Lord—
Lord, not my will but thine be done.
In the Name of thy Holy Son,
I Pray—
Today.
Amen.

42

Jesus Goes With Me

Jesus goes with me day and night,
He is my eternal light.
He guides my every step
and is my constant help.

Day by day, along life's way,
for others to know Him, I pray.
Without Him I would be lost,
but His blood has paid the cost.

Many years have gone by
and I stop and breathe a sigh.
But there is work to do
until my dash is through!

October 5, 1928 – …

—Del Aven

Something marvelous happens when we lift up our voice in the sacrifice of praise and thanksgiving ...

Count YOUR many blessings
Name them one by one,
And it will surprise you
What the Lord hath done!

****

Oh, taste and see that the LORD is good;
Blessed is the man who trusts in Him!
—Psalm 34:8

****

For additional information:

Blessings Through The Years
P.O. Drawer 269
Smithville, Mississippi 38870

www.blessingsthroughtheyears.com